Copyright

© 2024 Nitya N Tupili

All rights reserved. No part of this publication may be reproduced, distributed, or transmitted in any form or by any means, including photocopying, recording, or other electronic or mechanical methods, without the prior written permission of the author, except in the case of brief quotations embodied in critical reviews and certain other noncommercial uses permitted by copyright law.

This ebook is licensed for your personal enjoyment only. This ebook may not be re-sold or given away to other people. If you would like to share this book with another person, please purchase an additional copy for each recipient. If you're reading this book and did not purchase it, or it was not purchased for your use only, then please return to your favorite ebook retailer and purchase your own copy. Thank you for respecting the hard work of this author.

This book is a work of nonfiction. The information contained herein is intended for educational and informational purposes only. The author has made every effort to ensure the accuracy and completeness of the information provided. However, the author disclaims any liability for errors, omissions, or any perceived slights of specific persons, peoples, or organizations.

The examples and case studies presented in this book are based on the author's experiences and are used for illustrative purposes only. Any resemblance to actual persons, living or dead, or actual events is purely coincidental.

Published by **Nitya N Tupili**

First Ebook Edition : April 2024

Dedication

To my beloved parents, Suri Babu Tupili and Padma Latha Tupili,
Your unwavering love, support, and guidance have been the foundation of my life and the driving force behind my every achievement. You have always believed in me, even when I doubted myself, and your constant encouragement has given me the strength to pursue my dreams fearlessly.

From my earliest memories, you have instilled in me the values of hard work, perseverance, and integrity. You have taught me to face challenges head-on, to learn from my failures, and to celebrate my successes with humility and gratitude. Your wisdom and life lessons have shaped me into the person I am today.

Throughout my career journey, you have been my most ardent cheerleaders, my trusted advisors, and my unwavering support system. Your faith in me has been a constant source of motivation, pushing me to strive for excellence in all that I do.

This book is a testament to the incredible upbringing you have given me and the values you have ingrained in me. It is a reflection of the love, sacrifices, and countless opportunities you have provided me throughout my life. Without your support, this achievement would not have been possible.

I dedicate this book to you, Suri Babu Tupili and Padma Latha Tupili, as a token of my deepest gratitude and love. Your influence on my life has been immeasurable, and I am forever thankful for the gift of having you as my parents.

With all my love and appreciation,
Nitya N Tupili

Table of Contents

Copyright	1
Dedication	2
Table of Contents	3
Foreword	4
Preface	6
Acknowledgements	8
Introduction	9
Chapter 1: Defining Your Career Story	19
Chapter 2: Structuring Your Resume for Impact	35
Chapter 3: Crafting Compelling Experience Sections	49
Chapter 4: Enhancing With Additional Sections	73
Chapter 5: Polishing and Perfecting Your Resume	86
Chapter 6: Complements to Your Written Resume	99
Chapter 7: Navigating the Job Application Process	108
Conclusion	124
Epilogue: Your Career Journey Continues	126

Foreword

By Anika Kapoor, Successful Entrepreneur and Business Leader

In the ever-evolving landscape of the modern workforce, the ability to craft a compelling career story has become an indispensable skill. Your resume is not merely a document; it is a powerful narrative that captures the essence of your professional journey, showcasing your unique talents, achievements, and potential.

As a successful entrepreneur and business leader, I have witnessed firsthand the transformative impact of a well-crafted resume. It is the gateway to unlocking new opportunities, forging meaningful connections, and propelling your career to greater heights. In today's competitive job market, a compelling resume can be the difference between standing out and fading into obscurity.

"Resume Mastery: Unlocking the Secrets to a Compelling Career Story" is an invaluable resource that empowers you to take control of your professional narrative. This book goes beyond the conventional wisdom of resume writing, delving into the art of storytelling and personal branding. It equips you with the tools to weave your experiences, skills, and aspirations into a captivating tale that resonates with potential employers and opens doors to new possibilities.

Throughout my career, I have learned that success is not merely a matter of talent or qualifications; it is about effectively communicating your value proposition and showcasing your unique strengths. This book provides a roadmap to achieving just that, guiding you through the intricacies of crafting a resume that not only highlights your accomplishments but also reveals the depth of your character, passions, and potential.

Whether you are a recent graduate embarking on your first career journey, a seasoned professional seeking new challenges, or an entrepreneur exploring uncharted territories, this book offers invaluable insights and practical strategies to elevate your personal brand and position yourself for success.

In the pages that follow, you will discover the secrets to crafting a resume that captivates, inspires, and leaves a lasting impression. You will learn to harness the power of storytelling, leveraging your unique experiences and accomplishments to create a narrative that resonates with your target audience.

Embrace the wisdom and guidance within these pages, and embark on a transformative journey toward Resume Mastery. Unlock the secrets to a compelling career story, and watch as new doors of opportunity open before you, propelling you towards the professional fulfillment you deserve.

Preface

Writing this book, "Unlocking the Secrets of Resume Mastery," has been a true labor of love and a culmination of my years of experience as a career coach and HR professional. Throughout my career, I have witnessed countless talented individuals struggle to effectively showcase their skills and accomplishments on their resumes, often holding them back from reaching their full potential. This realization ignited a passion within me to help job seekers unlock the power of their unique career stories and create resumes that truly stand out in today's competitive job market.

In this book, I aim to provide you with a comprehensive, step-by-step guide to crafting a compelling resume that authentically represents your value proposition and helps you land your dream job. By sharing insights gained from my extensive experience working with diverse clients across various industries, I hope to demystify the resume-writing process and equip you with the tools and strategies needed to create a document that effectively communicates your unique strengths and accomplishments.

Throughout the following chapters, we will delve into the art of personal branding, the science of resume formatting, and the power of storytelling to create a resume that not only showcases your skills and experience but also captures the attention of hiring managers and recruiters. We will explore the importance of tailoring your resume to specific job opportunities, leveraging keywords to optimize for applicant tracking systems, and using complementary tools like cover letters and LinkedIn profiles to reinforce your professional brand.

But this book is not just about the technical aspects of resume writing. It's also about empowering you to take control of your career narrative and confidently articulate your unique value proposition. By embarking on this journey of self-discovery and reflection, you will gain a deeper understanding of your career goals, your transferable skills, and the unique experiences that have shaped you as a professional.

Whether you are a recent graduate just starting your career, a seasoned professional looking to make a career transition, or someone returning to the workforce after a break, this book is designed to meet you where you are and provide you with the guidance and support you need to create a resume that truly showcases your potential.

I have poured my heart and soul into this book, drawing upon my extensive knowledge and experience to create a resource that I hope will make a meaningful difference in your career journey. I am excited to share my insights with you and help you unlock the secrets of resume mastery.

So, let's dive in and begin the transformative process of crafting a resume that will open doors to new opportunities and help you achieve your professional goals. Together, we will create a document that not only showcases your past accomplishments but also positions you for a bright and successful future.

Acknowledgements

First and foremost, I want to express my deepest gratitude to my family and friends for their unwavering support and encouragement throughout the writing process of this book. Your belief in me and this project kept me motivated, even during the most challenging times.

I would also like to extend my sincere appreciation to the self-publishing platforms and resources that made this journey possible. The user-friendly tools and supportive communities have been invaluable in bringing this book to life.

To the countless authors whose works have inspired and influenced me over the years, I am forever indebted. Your words have been the fuel that ignited my passion for storytelling and motivated me to embark on this literary adventure.

Finally, to my readers, thank you for taking the time to delve into this book. Your interest and support mean more to me than you can imagine. I hope that the pages that follow will not only entertain but also inspire and resonate with you in profound ways.

Introduction

In today's highly competitive job market, your resume is often the first and potentially only opportunity to make a powerful impression on a potential employer. A well-crafted resume can open doors and secure interviews, while a poorly constructed one may relegate you to the rejection pile before you even have a chance to showcase your true talents and value.

The resume is more than just a list of your work experiences and education – it is the platform to tell your unique professional story in a way that resonates with employers and differentiates you from other candidates. An effective resume doesn't simply state your job duties, it highlights your key achievements, transferable skills, and the meaningful impact you've made in past roles.

At its core, resume mastery is about storytelling – crafting a cohesive narrative that markets your personal brand and demonstrates a clear fit for the opportunities you're pursuing. It requires taking a strategic approach to decide what to include, what to emphasize, and how to best position yourself for the roles that excite you most.

This book will serve as your comprehensive guide to unlocking the secrets of an extraordinary resume that doesn't just list your credentials, but paints a vivid picture of the value you have to offer an organization. You'll learn to define your distinctive career story, structure and format content for maximum impact, and create a compelling professional snapshot that motivates employers to schedule interviews.

We'll explore techniques for showcasing your achievements with powerful, quantified statements that demonstrate the scope of your skills in a tangible way. You'll gain insights into optimizing your resume for both human readers and Applicant Tracking Systems (ATS), ensuring your materials make it through the initial screening process. We'll cover tailoring strategies for customizing your resume for different roles, industries and companies.

In addition to the core written resume, we'll examine complementary self-marketing tools like cover letters, LinkedIn profiles, and personal websites that can reinforce your unique brand. You'll learn tips for navigating the entire job application process seamlessly – from customizing materials to preparing for interviews and negotiating offers successfully.

Whether you're a recent graduate launching your career, an experienced professional looking to transition industries, or simply ready to take your resume to new heights, this book will equip you with the tools and mindset to create a truly compelling career story that opens doors to rewarding opportunities.

By mastering the nuances of resume writing and positioning yourself as a standout candidate, you can take control of your professional journey and unlock the job and life you deserve. The path to resume excellence begins here – get ready to captivate employers and propel your career forward.

This book is divided into seven chapters that will comprehensively cover all aspects of crafting an extraordinary resume and positioning yourself for success throughout the job search process.

Chapter 1 lays the critical foundation by guiding you through defining your unique career story. We'll explore conducting a thorough self-assessment to identify your core values, interests, skills and accomplishments. You'll learn how to pinpoint your distinct value proposition and shape a personal brand that differentiates you.

In Chapter 2, we'll dive into the structural and formatting elements that ensure your resume is visually impactful and reader-friendly. You'll gain insights into choosing the ideal resume format, creating a strong header and profile summary, and optimizing each section for maximum readability. We'll also cover strategies for meeting the formatting requirements of applicant tracking systems.

Chapters 3 and 4 form the heart of the book, focused on transforming your work experience into compelling evidence of your qualifications. You'll master the art of crafting high-impact achievement statements that quantify and qualify the scope of your contributions. We'll break down how to select the most relevant details to include and techniques for highlighting transferable skills when changing careers. You'll also learn best practices for showcasing other key areas like education, skills and certifications.

In Chapter 5, you'll learn valuable tips for polishing and perfecting your resume to ensure clear, consistent and error-free content. We'll troubleshoot common pitfalls and mistakes that can undermine your materials. You'll also gain insights into tailoring your resume strategically for different roles and companies to maximize relevance.

While the core resume is crucial, Chapter 6 explores complementary tools like cover letters, LinkedIn profiles and personal websites that allow you to expand on your qualifications and amplify your professional brand. We'll dive into tactics for leveraging these resources to reinforce your strengths and unique selling points.

Finally, Chapter 7 will equip you with a roadmap for navigating the entire job application process smoothly. You'll learn strategies for customizing materials for each opportunity, following up effectively, preparing for interviews and ultimately, negotiating job offers with confidence. This chapter aims to provide a comprehensive approach to position you optimally every step of the way.

By the end of this book, you'll have a deep understanding of how to craft an extraordinary, high-impact resume that authentically markets your skills and positions you for exciting roles aligned with your career vision. You'll be empowered with tools, templates and mindset shifts to create a compelling career narrative that motivates employers and propels you along your desired professional path.

The journey to resume mastery is one of self-discovery, strategy and confident self-promotion. It requires understanding your unique strengths, purposefully shaping how you present yourself, and maintaining courage and resilience throughout the process. This book is designed to be your guide in that transformative journey toward career fulfillment.

While the idea of "selling yourself" on paper can feel daunting, this book will provide you with a roadmap for promoting your qualifications with authenticity and impact. You'll learn how to strike the right balance between confidence and humility, candor and professionalism.

Resumes are often viewed as a formulaic requirement, but the most effective ones do much more than checkboxes. A truly masterful resume goes beyond listing job duties – it tells a story that intrigues readers and makes them want to learn more about you as a candidate. It paints a clear, cohesive picture of the value you offer and your potential to make valuable contributions.

One of the keys to resume mastery is developing a deep self-awareness about your talents, motivations and the unique threads that have shaped your career journey so far. This book will guide you through exercises to gain clarity about the skills and experiences that make you distinctly qualified for the roles you covet.

With those insights, you'll be able to purposefully craft compelling content that positions you as an ideal fit. You'll learn techniques for making your achievements shine in quantifiable ways that convey tangible impact. You'll gain tools for creating a cohesive, focused narrative that targets your job search and marketing efforts.

Importantly, we'll also explore strategies for future-proofing your resume and keeping it updated in an ever-evolving career landscape. The job search process is rarely linear, so you'll need to be prepared to customize and adapt your materials for different opportunities over time.

Ultimately, this book is designed not just to help you secure your next job, but to provide you with resume mastery skills that will benefit you for years to come as you navigate changes and advancement. You'll be able to confidently market yourself and continue updating your compelling career story at every stage.

The path to resume excellence is a journey of professional development, self-discovery and embracing the mindset of a marketing specialist for your unique brand. It requires an investment of time and self-reflection, but the rewards of a fulfilling career make it worthwhile.

So let's get started! Turn the page and get ready to unlock the secrets to captivating employers and standing out as a truly compelling candidate. Resume mastery awaits.

One of the most empowering aspects of resume mastery is realizing that you have agency over how your career story is told. Your resume doesn't have to be a static list of job descriptions assigned by others. When crafted strategically, it allows you to shape the narrative and decide which details to emphasize or downplay based on your goals.

Throughout this book, you'll learn to become the author of your own professional journey. You'll gain techniques for analyzing roles through a different lens to extract impactful accomplishments and contributions that may have previously been overlooked or understated. You'll discover how to artfully construct your experiences into a coherent, compelling through-line.

The ability to control the messaging around your background is incredibly valuable, especially when pivoting to a new industry or transitioning between roles that may seem unrelated on the surface. Resume mastery empowers you to draw connections and repackage your skills in an authentic way that resonates with prospective employers.

At its core, this process is about developing an entrepreneurial mindset when it comes to managing your career. You'll learn to think strategically about long-term goals, identify target opportunities, research companies and roles thoroughly, and market yourself as the solution to their needs.

This book is designed not just to provide tactics, but to inspire you to view yourself as a CEO of your own career trajectory. You are the chief storyteller, marketer and business developer for your personal brand. Crafting a masterful resume is an exercise in taking ownership over your professional future.

With this foundation of skills and mindset shifts, you'll be equipped to confidently navigate the job search process on your own terms. You'll understand how to continue evolving your resume and personal marketing materials as your career progresses, keeping your story dynamic and relevant.

The journey of resume mastery ultimately leads to empowerment – over how you're perceived, the opportunities you attract, and your ability to achieve the career you envision. It's a process of unlocking your potential by taking full control over what makes your background unique and compelling.

If you're ready to invest in this transformative process and emerge as the leader of your own career narrative, then let's dive in. The secrets to resume mastery and the professional future you deserve await.

While the focus of this book is on crafting an extraordinary resume, it's important to note that your resume is just one piece of a comprehensive self-marketing strategy. In today's digital age, employers are looking beyond the traditional one-page document to gain a multidimensional understanding of candidates.

As we'll explore in later chapters, your resume works in concert with other career branding elements like your cover letter, LinkedIn profile, portfolio or personal website. This ecosystem of professional materials allows you to expand on different aspects of your background and qualifications in a nuanced way.

The masterful resume you'll create through this book will serve as the foundational cornerstone. However, you'll also learn how to leverage complementary resources to reinforce your unique value proposition and give prospective employers a well-rounded perspective on what you bring to the table.

By taking a cohesive approach that aligns your motivations, strengths and future goals, you'll be able to articulate a consistent and authentic professional brand across multiple channels and touchpoints. This unified narrative will ensure you're putting your best foot forward throughout the interview process.

Ultimately, landing your dream job is about more than just writing a great resume. It requires developing self-awareness, marketing savvy, resilience in the face of rejection, and the confidence to boldly sell your unique combination of skills and experiences.

This book will equip you with a comprehensive strategy for all of those elements. You'll gain clarity on identifying the right opportunities that excite you. You'll learn proven tactics for navigating every stage of the application process with poise – from submitting customized materials to acing interviews to negotiating offers.

By the end, you'll emerge with a renewed sense of control over your professional future and the tools to propel yourself towards rewarding, fulfilling work. You'll be able to approach your career journey as the leader, taking ownership over how your talents and ambitions are presented.

The road to resume mastery is a transformative one. It's a process of developing unshakable self-confidence, learning to tell your story in an authentic and compelling way, and unlocking your ability to attract opportunities aligned with your vision.

If you're ready to start that journey and take charge of your career trajectory, keep reading. The secrets to crafting an extraordinary career narrative are waiting to be unveiled.

Before we dive into the practical strategies and exercises, it's important to address a common mindset hurdle - the idea that crafting an impressive resume requires embellishment or exaggeration. This book rejects that flawed notion entirely. True resume mastery is about highlighting your authentic achievements and qualifications with clarity and impact.

At no point will you be encouraged to misrepresent your background or skills. In fact, one of the core principles is learning to let your accomplishments and strengths speak for themselves without needing to inflate or overstate. You'll develop techniques for weaving an engaging, compelling narrative using only the facts.

Embellishing ultimately undermines the entire purpose of an effective resume - to market yourself as an ideal candidate that a company would be excited and fortunate to hire. Deception erodes trust from the outset and puts you at risk of being perceived as inauthentic down the line. It's simply not worth jeopardizing your professional reputation. The most masterful resumes don't need to rely on puffery or hyperbole. When properly crafted with quantified details, focused formatting, and a coherent career narrative, your true qualifications and potential will shine through. This book will show you how to create that level of resonance and impact through honest storytelling alone.

Additionally, we'll explore strategies for adeptly addressing issues like employment gaps, frequent job changes, or transferring from different industries. You'll learn thoughtful ways to frame your experiences that get ahead of potential concerns while accentuating the positives through your unique lens.

The path to resume mastery is one of embracing and promoting your background with confidence - owning your narrative and presenting yourself skillfully, not needing to overcompensate through embellishment. This book is designed to provide you with ethical, trustworthy guidance for achieving that level of self-assurance.

By avoiding gimmicks and favoring truthful storytelling, you'll create resume materials that highlight your qualifications with substance and authenticity. You'll be able to interview with the poise of knowing your credentials were marketed accurately from the start. And most importantly, you'll be able to accept your next role with the integrity and professionalism it deserves.

So let's begin the journey of unlocking your ability to craft a truly compelling career narrative that opens doors to rewarding opportunities. The first step is developing a deep understanding of your unique strengths, backstory, and future ambitions. With that self-knowledge as the foundation, you'll be able to create extraordinary resume materials that market your talents powerfully and authentically. Resume mastery awaits! As you prepare to delve into the step-by-step guidance this book provides, it's important to keep an open mindset and be prepared for self-reflection. The process of resume mastery requires taking an honest inventory of your experiences, skills, accomplishments and future goals.

You may uncover new insights about yourself that reshape how you view your career journey so far. You'll likely identify hidden gems, overlooked achievements and transferred abilities that deserve to be highlighted more prominently in your professional narrative.

Embrace this self-discovery process with vulnerability and curiosity. Be willing to challenge your own assumptions about what makes you marketable. The goal is to emerge with a clarified vision of your unique value proposition and brand.

Throughout the book, you'll have opportunities to reassess your priorities, pinpoint your driving motivations and ambitions, and realign your career trajectory if needed. This level of self-awareness is what allows you to craft a truly compelling career story tailored for the roles and companies that excite you most.

You'll also be pushed to step outside your comfort zone when it comes to confidently promoting your strengths and qualifications. For many, the idea of brazenly "selling yourself" doesn't come naturally. But resume mastery requires developing the mindset and skills of an entrepreneur marketing their most valuable product - themselves.

This book will provide guidance for finding the balance between confidence and humility in self-promotion. You'll learn how to quantify accomplishments, craft powerful achievement statements, and thoughtfully discuss your background during interviews. With practice, advocating for yourself becomes second nature.

Ultimately, resume mastery is about developing a profound sense of self-assuredness in your unique abilities and potential. It's a process of overcoming self-doubt, impostor syndrome, and barriers to self-promotion. You'll finish this book with renewed agency over your professional future and career trajectory.

So get ready to embark on a journey of self-discovery, authentic storytelling, and strategic marketing of your talents. Prepare to unlock a new level of confidence and take full control over how your compelling career narrative is crafted and shared with prospective employers.

The path to resume excellence begins now. The strategies that follow will provide you with a comprehensive guide to crafting extraordinary career marketing materials and positioning yourself as a top candidate. But first, you must commit to doing the self-work required to truly master your professional story. The rewards of career fulfillment and exciting opportunities await those willing to invest in this transformative process.

Let's begin!

Chapter 1: Defining Your Career Story

Before you can craft an extraordinary resume that markets you as a top candidate, you must first have a clear understanding of your unique career narrative. Defining your professional story begins with a deep process of self-discovery and articulating the key elements that make your background distinctive.

In this chapter, you'll conduct a thorough self-assessment to identify your core values, interests, skills and accomplishments. You'll use these insights to pinpoint your personal brand and unique value proposition as an employee. And you'll learn to synthesize these building blocks into compelling career summary and objective statements that will hook prospective employers.

The Self-Assessment: Uncovering Your Foundations

To shape an authentic career narrative, you must first gain clarity about the enduring motivations and traits that have guided your professional path so far. This self-inventory process will illuminate the throughlines and consistencies that make your journey uniquely yours.

Values Assessment

What principles, ethics and ideals are most important to you in a workplace? Examples could include integrity, innovation, work-life balance, autonomy, or collaboration. Identify your top 5 values and provide examples of how they've influenced your decisions.

Interests Inventory

What type of work actually excites and energizes you? List areas you're passionate about, subjects you're inherently curious about, and tasks/projects you find intrinsically motivating and rewarding.

Skills Profiling

Outline your full skills inventory - both technical/hard skills (e.g. coding languages, software, certifications) and portable/soft skills (e.g. communication, problem-solving, leadership). Group them into categories and indicate your levels of proficiency.

Accomplishments Review

Make a list of your career accomplishments so far - projects you've excelled in, challenges you've overcome, impressive results you've produced. Don't filter yet, just do a brain dump of potential achievements to explore further.

This foundational self-assessment provides the raw materials to construct your career narrative. By reflecting on your values, interests, skills and accomplishments, you start to see consistencies, strengths and patterns emerge that can be woven into a compelling story.

Identifying Your Unique Value Proposition

With your self-assessment complete, the next step is to analyze your inventory of traits and experiences to pinpoint your unique value proposition to potential employers. What specific mix of skills, accomplishments and perspectives do you offer that would make you an invaluable asset?

To uncover your unique value proposition, look for ways your background differentiates you and tells a distinctive narrative:
- Identify skills & experiences that are rare combinations
- Note ways you've crossed disciplines/functions/industries
- Pinpoint times you were entrepreneurial or innovated new solutions
- List times you took initiative or leadership beyond your role
- Highlight ways you solved challenging or complex problems
- Determine what value-adds you contribute beyond core job duties

Your value proposition should be grounded in specific, provable examples and accomplishments from your experience. It should position you as someone who can deliver unique forms of impact that few other candidates can match.

For example, your value proposition could be: "Blend of digital marketing and data analytics expertise allows me to optimize campaigns with a scientific, metrics-driven approach." Or "Cross-functional project management experience combined with coding abilities enables me to bridge technical and operational gaps."

Shaping Your Personal Brand

With your unique value proposition defined, the next step is to craft an overarching personal brand narrative that captures the essence of who you are as a professional.

Your personal brand should encompass:
- Your skills, strengths and key experiences/accomplishments.
- Your values and what's important to you in a role/company.
- The types of problems/challenges you're motivated to solve.
- Your future goals and ambitions for impact and growth.

To develop your brand, create a brand positioning statement that captures your value proposition and professional persona in 1-2 concise sentences:
"A data-driven digital marketer motivated to drive revenue growth through scientific campaign optimization and innovative ad strategies."
"Versatile project leader adept at uniting cross functional teams behind delivering complex, technical solutions that exceed client needs."
This brand statement should convey what makes you distinctly qualified and the value you can provide. It articulates your competitive advantage and foreshadows the strengths you'll emphasize in your resume's career summary.

Crafting a Compelling Career Summary

The career summary (also called a professional summary or qualifications summary) is one of the most critical elements of your resume. This 3-5 sentence introduction needs to quickly capture attention and motivate employers to keep reading about your background.

An effective career summary powerfully encapsulates your personal brand narrative. It highlights your unique value proposition and marketable skills. It provides a high-level preview of the strengths and accomplishments that will be expanded upon throughout the rest of your resume.

To craft a compelling career summary:

1. Review your personal brand positioning statement and value proposition. Identify 3-4 core strengths, skills or accomplishments you want to emphasize.
2. Open with a concise, high-impact statement that immediately conveys your value:
   "Data-driven digital marketer driving revenue growth through..."
   "Innovative project leader known for delivering technical solutions that..."
3. Incorporate select keywords and hard/technical skills relevant for your target roles.
4. Quantify accomplishments with impressive numbers/metrics when possible:
   "Increased email open rates by 25% through A/B testing and segmentation tactics."
   "Spearheaded $2M cloud migration project with <5% downtime..."
5. Highlight transferable skills and frame experiences in a future-focused way:
   "Extensive background leading cross-functional teams..."
   "Proven history optimizing processes to maximize efficiency/productivity..."
6. Aim for a confident yet humble tone. Sell yourself but avoid overblown claims.

Example Career Summaries:

"Data-driven digital marketer driving revenue growth through scientific campaign optimization, innovative ad strategies and immersive brand storytelling. Blend of analytics expertise and creative mindset for launching customer-centric, ROI-positive initiatives that capture audience engagement."

"Innovative project leader known for spearheading technical solutions that exceed client needs and business objectives. Proven expertise uniting cross-functional teams behind delivering complex, high-stakes initiatives on accelerated timelines. Passionate about leveraging emerging technologies to solve operational challenges."

Your career summary is your first opportunity to capture attention and establish fit. It should provide a concise yet compelling snapshot of your background and the unique value you can offer as an employee. With a well-crafted summary leading the way, the rest of your resume will substantiate and expand upon those introductory brand pillars.

Defining Your Career Objectives

In addition to a powerful career summary, your resume should also incorporate a 1-2 sentence career objective or qualifications summary tailored for your current goals. This focused statement provides context about your motivations and desired trajectory.

For example, objectives could look like:

- "Seeking opportunity to leverage digital marketing and data analytics expertise to drive customer engagement and revenue growth."
- "Strategic leader looking to join a fast-paced technical startup environment to spearhead innovative cloud computing initiatives."

This career objective gives the reader a clear understanding of how to view your background and qualifications through the lens of your immediate professional aspirations. It also allows you to incorporate relevant keywords for your job search.

The objective should align with the personal brand and strengths highlighted in your career summary. Together, these introductory sections establish a cohesive, focused narrative about your skills and future fit right from the start.

Determining the Most Relevant Details

With your personal brand platform and career objectives solidified, the final step of defining your story involves pinpointing the most relevant and compelling details from your professional and academic experiences to include in your resume.

Not every accomplishment or skill needs to make it onto the page. The goal is to curate and elevate only the qualifications that reinforce your unique value proposition and align with your current career goals.

Here are some guidelines for selecting the most relevant details to include:
- Focus on achievements, skills and experiences that differentiate you as a candidate and ladder up to your core strengths.
- Analyze past roles through the lens of transferable skills that could be applicable to future opportunities.
- Emphasize scope, scale and impact when highlighting accomplishments. Use quantifiable metrics to tangibly illustrate results.
- Only include credentials, affiliations and activities that are directly applicable and enhance your qualifications.
- If changing roles/industries, reframe experiences with that career transition in mind.
- Don't undersell seemingly unrelated skills.

The accomplishments and skills you choose to feature should support and reinforce the professional narrative you've defined through your personal brand, career summary and objectives. With a focused, cohesive story taking shape, you're ready to begin structuring and drafting an extraordinary resume.

Auditing Your Career Journey

A critical step in the self-assessment process is taking an honest inventory of your professional experiences so far. This allows you to identify potential gaps, pivots or evolutions in your narrative that may need framing.

As part of this audit, map out a chronological timeline of your career history with the following details:
- Job titles and tenures at each role
- Key responsibilities and achievements
- Skills developed or utilized
- Reasons for staying or leaving roles
- Transitions between roles/industries

As you review this chronology, look for any potential derailers or inconsistencies that could raise red flags to employers. This may include job-hopping, prolonged employment gaps, lack of promotions/growth or transitions that seem like career tangents.

The key is to get ahead of those perceived concerns by developing thoughtful ways to frame your journey through the lens of your defined career story.
For example:

- Identify themes or throughlines that connect each role
- Reframe employment gaps as strategic periods of development
- Highlight transferable skills that made transitions logical

- Note any entrepreneurial experience or personal motivators
- Explain reasons for pivots in a future-focused way

With a clear understanding of your career path's chronology, you can craft a cohesive walk that markets your background in the most compelling, progressive way aligned with your goals.

Uncovering Your "Greatest Hits"

As part of your accomplishments review, go a level deeper to uncover your most impressive, quantifiable "greatest hits" that deserve premium real estate on your resume.

These achievements could include:
- Revenue/profit/sales numbers you increased
- Costs you reduced through process improvements
- Major projects or initiatives you led from conception
- New systems, policies or technologies you implemented
- Challenges or problems you overcame in innovative ways

For each "greatest hit", validate the tangible, measurable impact you made through numbers and metrics. Quantify the scale, scope, and results as concretely as possible.

For example:

- "Restructured sales territories and optimized coverage models to drive 35% YOY revenue growth and $18M in new business."
- "Spearheaded ERP system implementation across 14 global locations, achieving 22% increase in operational efficiency."
- "Overhauled customer support workflow reducing response times by 62% and contributing to 18% annual revenue retention."

These hard-hitting, data-backed accomplishments provide irrefutable proof of the level of impact and value you can deliver as an employee. They bring your core strengths and personal brand narrative to life in tangible ways.

As you're defining your career story, these achievements will likely emerge as the anchors and highlights you'll want to strategically feature throughout your resume. Use them as guiding stars for shaping your professional narrative around the skills and experiences that enabled those impressive outcomes.

Tying It All Together

By completing the self-assessment, personal branding and "greatest hits" exercises in this chapter, you've now built a solid foundation for crafting an authentic, compelling career narrative that positions you as a uniquely qualified candidate.

You've clarified your skills and interests through a personal inventory. You've defined a powerful value proposition that differentiates you. You've shaped an overarching personal brand narrative that conveys your professional persona. You've crafted a high-impact career summary and objective statement to hook readers. And you've identified the most relevant accomplishments and details to strategically showcase.

With this comprehensive suite of personal marketing materials and storyline developed, you now have a clear blueprint for constructing extraordinary resume content that advances your goals. You understand what makes you unique, what value you offer to employers, and how to market your background persuasively.

In the next chapter, we'll explore strategies for structuring and formatting your resume to optimally present this compelling career narrative in a reader-friendly, visually-impactful way. But first, take a moment to review and internalize the personal brand platform and storyline you've defined for yourself here.

You've unlocked the foundational building blocks of resume mastery - a profound sense of self-awareness, the ability to shape your authentic narrative, and the confidence to promote your strengths strategically. Bringing this career story to life on paper is the next critical step to open doors.

Identifying Your Career Vision

While much of this chapter has focused on conducting a self-assessment to define your past experiences and current qualifications, it's also important to have a clear vision for where you want your career to go next.

Without this future-focused perspective, it becomes more difficult to strategically position your background and craft a narrative that resonates for your desired roles and opportunities.

As part of the self-discovery process, take some time to reflect on your long-term ambitions and aspirations:

- What type of roles/responsibilities most excite and motivate you?
- What kind of company culture or work environment aligns with your values?
- What are your goals for professional growth and development?
- What types of challenges are you interested in tackling?
- What level of impact or seniority are you aiming for long-term?

Get descriptive and imagine your ideal scenarios 5-10 years into the future. What does success look and feel like for you? What are you hoping to experience and accomplish? This exercise allows you to reverse-engineer the skills and experiences you'll need to acquire or emphasize in order to make that career vision a reality. It provides direction for how you'll want to strategically market yourself through your resume and other professional branding materials.

For example, if your goal is to eventually run digital marketing operations for a major consumer brand, you'll want to craft a narrative highlighting your abilities to:
- Develop innovative, data-driven campaign strategies at scale
- Manage and lead high-performing, cross-functional teams
- Utilize latest marketing automation and measurement technologies
- Analyze and interpret consumer data/insights to drive decisions
- Proven track record of hitting ambitious revenue and ROI metrics

With that clear career vision in mind, you can thoughtfully mine your past experiences to elevate relevant accomplishments and transferable skills that ladder up to that future goal.

Identifying Your Passion Projects

In addition to your professional experiences, take inventory of any personal or side projects you've been involved with that allow you to showcase additional skills and interests. These "passion projects" can be powerful resume differentiators.

They demonstrate your ability to take initiative, embrace new challenges, and invest effort toward personal and professional growth. Highlighting these experiences can reinforce your personal brand and add dimension to your overall narrative.

Some examples of passion project areas to include:
- Volunteer experiences or pro-bono consulting work
- Participation in professional associations or groups
- Examples of public speaking, teaching or mentoring
- Personal blogs, podcasts or published writing you've created
- Online courses, certifications or training you've completed
- Coding projects, apps or websites you've built
- Entrepreneurial or side business ventures you've launched

As you're defining your career story, look for connections between your passion projects and your core qualifications that could be woven together. These outside pursuits can sometimes elevate abilities that weren't fully utilized in your traditional job roles.

For example, if you want to transition into digital marketing, you could emphasize:
"My personal passion for food and restaurant blogging allowed me to hone skills in content creation, SEO, social media marketing and Google Analytics analysis - all of which I'm excited to bring into a professional digital marketing role."

By thoughtfully integrating these passion projects into your career narrative, you create a multi-dimensional professional persona beyond just your core work experiences. It allows you to craft a more well-rounded, memorable personal brand.

Identifying Your Differentiated Differentiators

As you craft your career narrative, it's critical to pinpoint the specific skills, experiences and qualifications that allow you to genuinely differentiate yourself from other candidates. These are the components that make your background unique and give you a compelling edge.

To identify your "differentiated differentiators", look for ways your combination of abilities defies conventional categories or expectations for your roles. These could include:
• Bringing expertise from adjacent or unexpected disciplines
• Combining seemingly disparate skills in innovative ways
• Possessing rare technical capabilities for your field
• Bridging diverse roles, functions or perspectives
• Applying entrepreneurial thinking to drive new initiatives
• Tackling problems using creative or unorthodox approaches

For example, a differentiated differentiator could be:

- "My background in industrial engineering combined with coding abilities allowed me to overhaul the plant's legacy manufacturing workflow systems, automating processes to boost efficiency by 37%."

Or,

- "As a trained improviser, I'm able to bring high EQ leadership perspectives to drive team creativity, adaptability and innovative problem-solving."

These points of unique differentiation are powerful hooks that can capture employers' attention and imagination. They position you as a dynamic candidate who can add multidimensional value.

When defining your career story, make sure to showcase these differentiated differentiators prominently. They'll be critical for standing out in a crowded applicant pool and demonstrating how you can provide a unique impact.

Prepare to Tell Your Story

With all of the self-assessment, personal branding and career visioning work you've done in this chapter, you should now have a wealth of material and insights to craft an authentic, compelling career narrative. You understand your core values, interests and abilities. You've defined a powerful personal brand and value proposition. You've identified your greatest hits and differentiated qualifications. And you have a clear vision for where you want to take your professional journey next.

This foundational story work is what allows you to create a masterful resume - one that markets you as a cohesive, thematic candidate rather than just presenting a list of roles and responsibilities. Every section and accomplishment highlighted will tie back to your overarching career narrative in an intentional, strategic way.

As you prepare to start writing and structuring your resume content, keep your defined career story and personal brand pillars top of mind. Use them as a guiding light to ensure all of your written material ladders up to reinforcing your key strengths, qualifications and future vision.

You may also want to summarize your career story into a brief elevator pitch or narrative bio that you can easily customize and include in different scenarios throughout the job search process. Having these consolidated narratives allows you to consistently promote your background with clarity and impact.

Finally, be prepared to continue refining and adjusting your career story as needed. The personal branding you've done provides a solid foundation, but your narrative should remain dynamic and responsive as you navigate new opportunities, transitions and goals.

Defining your career story is an iterative process of building greater self-awareness over time. Embrace it as a journey of continual refinement and evolution as you and your ambitions grow. The exercises in this chapter have provided you with a thoughtful, multi-dimensional narrative to market yourself from. With that strong launch point established, you're ready to bring this authentic personal brand to life visually and strategically through your resume.

Key Takeaways:

• Crafting an extraordinary resume begins with conducting a deep self-assessment to identify your core values, interests, skills and standout accomplishments. This provides the raw material for your career narrative.
• Analyze your experiences to pinpoint your unique value proposition - the distinctive strengths and qualifications that differentiate you as a candidate.
• Shape an overarching personal brand narrative that conveys your professional persona, goals and the problems you're driven to solve.

- Develop a high-impact career summary and objective statement that hooks prospective employers and previews your brand pillars.
- Thoughtfully select only the most relevant accomplishments and details that reinforce your strengths and align with your current career trajectory.
- Craft your career narrative through the lens of your long-term vision and aspirations. Reverse-engineer the qualifications you'll need to market.
- Integrate passion projects and outside experiences that add dimension and transferable skills to your professional story.
- Identify unique "differentiated differentiators" that allow you to genuinely stand out from other candidates.
- Be prepared to continually refine and evolve your career narrative as you pursue new roles and opportunities over time.

By completing the personal branding and storyline exercises in this chapter, you've now built a solid foundation to craft an authentic, compelling career narrative that positions you strategically.

You understand what makes your background unique and the specific value you offer employers. You've defined the throughlines, skills and "greatest hits" accomplishments to feature prominently. And you have a clear vision for how you want to market yourself for future opportunities.

With this comprehensive self-awareness and career narrative developed, you can now apply an intentional, unified strategy as you structure the written content and formatting of your extraordinary resume. The personal brand pillars you've established will ensure every section conveys a cohesive, thematic presentation of your qualifications as an ideal candidate.

The journey of resume mastery starts with taking ownership in defining your own authentic career story from the inside-out. You've now completed that critical first step -

the rest of this book will show you how to bring that powerful narrative to life physically on paper and visually online.

Get ready to let your unique strengths as a candidate truly shine!

Chapter 2: Structuring Your Resume for Impact

With the critical work of defining your authentic career story and personal brand complete, it's time to turn those insights into a visually impactful, strategically crafted resume document. How your content is structured and formatted plays a huge role in grabbing employers' attention and creating a compelling, cohesive professional narrative.

In this chapter, you'll learn techniques for optimizing every aspect of your resume's construction - from choosing the ideal format to incorporating quantified accomplishments to tailoring for specific roles and Applicant Tracking Systems (ATS). You'll master best practices around layout, fonts, section ordering and more to ensure your extraordinary qualifications are packaged in a reader-friendly, polished way.

By applying an intentional, marketing-minded approach to your resume's structure and formatting, you can powerfully bring your personal brand to life on the page. You'll create a cohesive, thematic presentation aligned with your goals that motivates employers to seriously consider you as an ideal candidate.

Choosing the Ideal Resume Format

The first major structural decision is which resume format will work best for you based on your background and experience level - chronological, functional or combination.

A chronological resume lists your work experience in reverse chronological order, with your most recent role first. This is the most popular and conventional format, as it provides a clear career timeline and progression for the reader to follow.

Chronological resumes work well for those with a relatively linear career trajectory and continuous employment history. They allow you to showcase how you've been promoted or taken on increasing responsibility over time.

However, this format can also draw attention to any gaps in employment or frequent job changes. It may be less ideal for career changers whose experience doesn't directly translate to a new field.

A functional resume focuses more on highlighting your key skills and accomplishments grouped by category, rather than listing out every role chronologically. This format is strategic for those looking to transfer their qualifications to a new industry, as it allows you to draw connections between transferable skills from different experiences.

Functional resumes can also be effective for those returning to work after an extended absence, or who have gaps or career pivots that are difficult to explain in a chronological format. The emphasis is on your skills and abilities rather than linear job descriptions.

However, functional resumes are less common and may raise red flags for more conservative employers or Applicant Tracking Systems looking for a traditional chronological work history.

A combination resume provides a middle-ground approach by combining elements of chronological and functional formatting. It typically leads with a qualifications summary highlighting key skills and strengths, then provides a brief chronological work history section supplemented by detailed accomplishments regarded by skill categories.

Combination resumes allow you to draw attention to your most relevant qualifications through the functional section, while still providing a chronological work overview for more traditional employers. This balanced approach can work well for career changers, those with diverse experiences, or roles that require a wide mix of skills.

When deciding which format is best for your background and goals, consider:

- Your experience level and career trajectory so far

- Whether you need to explain any gaps or job changes
- If you are looking to transfer skills to a new role or industry
- The conventions and norms for your desired roles and field

Ultimately, the right format should optimize the way your strongest credentials and professional narrative shine through. Don't be afraid to strategically choose the approach that markets your qualifications most effectively.

Optimizing Your Header

While the header section may seem like a small component, it's one of the first things employers will notice when reviewing your resume. Optimizing these contact details to create a polished first impression is important.

Your header should include:
- Your full name - Consider using a slightly larger font size or bold formatting to make it stand out
- Your professional email address - Avoid outdated emails like Hotmail or emails containing inappropriate usernames
- Your phone number
- Your city and state of residence - You don't need to include a full street address
- Optional: A link to your LinkedIn profile or personal website/portfolio

For formatting, it's ideal to have your header information centered at the top of the page or aligned neatly to one side. Use a clean, consistent font that's easy to read.

You can also include a link to relevant social media accounts like Twitter or GitHub if they showcase your industry expertise or body of work. However, avoid listing personal social media accounts unless they are portfolios of your professional abilities.

If you are pursuing opportunities in multiple locations, you may want to remove the city and state and simply list your email and phone number to avoid raising red flags about relocation.

Overall, your header should have a polished, professional presentation that avoids any distracting personal information. It should make it easy for employers to contact you while establishing your resume's overall tone as a sleek, highly intentional marketing document.

Crafting an Impactful Profile or Qualifications Summary
After the header, your next opportunity to hook employers is through your profile or qualifications summary statement. This introductory paragraph (3-5 lines) should swiftly capture your "elevator pitch" and value proposition.

As covered in Chapter 1, your qualifications summary should encapsulate the core strengths and key personal brand pillars that make you an ideal candidate. It should entice employers to continue reading further by providing a thematic preview of your most relevant skills and impressive achievements.

Some best practices for writing an impactful qualifications summary:
• Lead with a powerful, high-level overview statement:
"Data-driven digital marketer driving revenue growth through..."
"Innovative project leader known for delivering technical solutions that..."
• Incorporate select keywords and hard skills relevant to your target roles
• Quantify where possible by highlighting impressive numbers/metrics:
"Increased email open rates by 25% through segmentation tactics."
"Spearheaded $2M cloud migration project with <5% downtime..."
• Emphasize transferable skills and frame experiences in a future-focused way:
"Proven expertise leading cross-functional teams and implementing operational efficiencies."

"Extensive background liaising with external partners and managing competing priorities."

• Aim for a confident yet grounded, professional tone. Avoid overblown claims or excessive humblebrags.

• Adjust length to be concise but substantive - most are 3-5 lines of precise, high-impact phrasing.

Your qualifications summary is your first opportunity to establish fit with the roles you're targeting. It should swiftly convey your unique value proposition and motivate employers to keep reading about your background and qualifications.

Determining the Ideal Section Order

After your header and qualifications summary, determining the ideal order for presenting the remaining sections of your resume is key for telling your professional narrative strategically.

For most candidates following a chronological format, the typical section order is:

- Header
- Qualifications Summary
- Professional Experience (or Work History)
- Education & Credentials
- Technical Skills or Additional Relevant Skills
- Additional Sections (Volunteer Work, Certifications, etc.)

This order is reader-friendly and follows a logical flow - it leads with a high-level overview of your qualifications, goes into the most important details about your work experiences and achievements, then provides supplemental information about your knowledge base, skills and other credentials.

However, you may want to prioritize section order differently based on your particular background and goals:

- If you have a particularly impressive academic pedigree, you could move your Education section closer to the top.

- For those making a career transition, you may want to place more emphasis on your Relevant Skills section over Chronological Experience to highlight your transferable qualifications.

Incorporating Accomplishments & Quantified Bullet Points

One of the most critical components for giving your resume true impact is incorporating quantified accomplishment statements and bullet points throughout your experience sections. This is how you backup your professional narrative with hard evidence and tangible results.

When listing out your responsibilities for each role, don't just provide bland job descriptions. Identify 3-5 key accomplishments, projects or improvements you spearheaded that allow you to showcase the scope of your contributions through numbers, metrics and quantifiable data.

For example, rather than listing a responsibility like "Managed email marketing campaigns", you could reframe it as an accomplishment:
"Overhauled email marketing campaigns using A/B testing and consumer data segmentation, increasing open rates by 25% and converting $180K in new sales pipeline."

See how that bullet point jumps off the page? It validates your experience with hard performance data and showcases the level of impact you can deliver for an employer.
Other examples of quantified accomplishment statements:
- "Implemented Lean Six Sigma methodology to streamline supply chain operations, reducing overheads by $325K annually."
- "Redesigned and launched an intuitive customer-facing portal increasing NPS scores by 27 points."

- "Mentor 6 entry-level developers, providing leadership and technical onboarding to boost ramp time by 40%."

As you describe your responsibilities, look for opportunities to frame them using concrete numbers, metrics, or quantifiable scope to illustrate scale and impact. This transforms your experience from vague claims into proven credibility.

You can also strategically incorporate keywords and hard skills into your accomplishment bullets, either by calling them explicitly or by describing how you applied those tools and abilities in context.

Overall, your goal should be for each role to have 3-5 quantified, achievement-oriented bullet points that showcase your potential value to a prospective employer through demonstrated results. This level of tangible, measurable evidence will give your resume undeniable impact.

Tailoring for Applicant Tracking Systems (ATS)

In today's age of automated hiring, many employers now use applicant tracking systems (ATS) to screen resumes before a human ever lays eyes on them. Optimizing your resume to make it through these ATS scans is critical.

Applicant tracking systems work by parsing resumes for relevant keywords related to required skills, credentials and experience for the roles they're hiring for. If your resume doesn't include enough of the right keywords and phrases, it may automatically be filtered out before getting in front of a recruiter.

Some tips for optimizing your resume to be ATS-friendly:

- Research common keywords and skills listings for your target roles and be sure to integrate them into your qualifications summaries and experience bullets naturally. Don't overstuff, but do include them at least 2-3 times.

- Use common headings and section titles like "Work Experience", "Skills", and "Education" to ensure the ATS can easily categorize your information.

- Stick to common fonts like Times New Roman or Arial that the ATS will be able to parse properly. Avoid intricate designs or formatting that could confuse the system.

- Save your resume as a .doc or .pdf file, as some ATS may not be able to read other file formats properly.

- Include relevant acronyms and industry terminology in context to demonstrate fluency.

- Use standard date formatting like "May 2018 - Present" so the ATS can interpret dates correctly.

You'll also want to be sure you're submitting a tailored resume customized for each specific role rather than sending a generic document. Many ATS flag and filter out resumes that don't contain enough precise keywords related to the job posting.

While you want your resume to be ATS-friendly, the content should still read naturally for human reviewers too. Strike a balance between strategic keyword integration and an easy-to-scan, logical presentation of your credentials.

Formatting and Layout Best Practices

The way your resume content is visually formatted and laid out on the page plays a huge role in its clarity, professionalism and overall reader experience. Maintaining consistent, clean formatting allows you to establish credibility while optimizing scannability.

Here are some key formatting and layout best practices:

Font Choice & Other Typography

- Choose a traditional, easy-to-read font like Arial, Times New Roman, Calibri or Georgia

- Keep font sizes between 10-12 pt for body text
- Use judicious emphasis with bold, italics and caps - but don't overdo it
- Maintain consistent font styles and formatting between sections

Page Margins & Spacing

- Keep margins between 0.5" to 1" on all sides
- Use single line spacing, with spacing between sections
- Separate section headings with horizontal lines to delineate
- Allow ample white space throughout to avoid dense walls of text

Section Ordering & Alignment

- Present sections in a logical order (Summary, Experience, Education, etc.)
- Align section titles and details consistently using tabs or indents
- Use reverse chronological order for listing experiences
- Align dates and details consistently for each role

Length & Formatting Extras

- Aim for a one-page resume when possible (two max for senior roles)
- Use bullet points, not paragraphs, to list out accomplishments
- You can integrate subtle pops of color, lines, borders if aligned with brand
- Leave out "References Available Upon Request" to save space

Overall, the goal of your formatting and layout should be to create an extremely clean, polished and visually digestible presentation. Guide the reader's eye easily through your content using consistent structure, styles and plenty of white space.

Avoid gimmicky designs or visuals that could come across as distracting or unprofessional. Let the substance of your qualifications and accomplishments speak for themselves through clear, intentional formatting.

Leveraging Visual Elements Effectively

While your resume should remain text-focused, you can selectively integrate some visual elements to enhance your content's impact and storytelling when appropriate. Charts, graphs, icons, process diagrams or other visuals can be powerful tools for quantifying scope or conveying context around key accomplishments.

For example, you could include a simple bar chart or graph to visualize revenue growth, cost savings, productivity improvements or other quantifiable achievements you've driven. This allows the employer to quickly digest those numbers in a high-impact, memorable way.

If you have technical expertise in areas like wireframing, design, code or data visualization, you could include some samples of your actual work as visual evidence of your skills in action. However, only include portfolio pieces that are relevant to the roles you're targeting.

You can also use icons or visual markers to concisely convey skills with software, tools or programming languages. But be sure to keep these visual elements minimal and uncluttered.

Some roles, like those in project management or operations, may benefit from visualizing complex processes or systems you've implemented using clean diagrams or workflow charts. These visuals can provide helpful context around the scope and impact of your work.

When incorporating any visual elements, be sure they are enhancing your resume's content rather than distracting or overwhelming it. The text should remain the primary focus, with visuals playing a supportive role in illustrating key points. If adding visuals, be sure to maintain plenty of blank space and simplicity in your layout.

Used strategically, some well-designed visuals can transform your resume from just dense text into a more interactive, memorable and quantifiable presentation of your capabilities. But take care not to go overboard and undermine your professional brand.

Reviewing for Consistency and Cohesive Narrative

The final step in structuring an impactful resume is thoroughly reviewing your content through a lens of consistency and ensuring it presents a cohesive, unified professional narrative aligned with your goals.

From your header to your qualifications summary to the way you've framed your experience sections, all of the elements should tie together thematically and reinforce your overarching personal brand. There should be a natural flow and progression guiding employers on your career journey.

Here are some areas to cross-check for consistency:
• Verify formatting and stylistic elements like font sizes, bolding, lines, spacing, etc. are aligned throughout
• Confirm dates, employer names, titles and other details are identical when repeated across sections
• Review your accomplishment statements and skills listed to ensure there is no contradictory information

Check that the lens or point of view you've framed experiences through is consistent with your stated goals and qualifications summary. For example, if you've highlighted project management abilities, have you carried that theme through each role?

Critically evaluate if there are any gaps, jumps or abrupt transitions in your narrative flow that don't make sense or could raise red flags for employers. If so, see if you can reframe or clarify those components to maintain a smoother, more cohesive storyline.
Ensure the skills, accomplishments and keywords you've integrated align with your target roles and the employers you'll be pursuing. There should be a crystal clear sense of the types of opportunities you're marketing yourself towards.

From a more subjective stance, read through your resume holistically as if you were an employer to evaluate if there is a clear, compelling personal brand that shines through thematically. Can you succinctly articulate the main value proposition and strengths being conveyed?

If not, revisit your qualifications summary and experience bullets to punch up that cohesive narrative in a more unified, intentional way. Your personal brand pillars should be woven throughout like a consistent thread.

Finally, be sure you don't have any glaring holes or missing pieces that could raise questions for employers. For example, if you have an employment gap listed without explanation or are lacking specific years for dated experiences, be sure to address those components either directly or in your cover letter.

Maintaining consistency, cohesion and a unified narrative flow is what transforms your resume from a flat list of credentials into a persuasive, impactful personal marketing statement. It's what allows employers to quickly grasp your thematic strengths and potential value while feeling like they have a comprehensive, truthful picture of what you bring to the table.

With a thorough review through this lens of consistency and cohesion, you can ensure your extraordinary qualifications are being presented in the most strategic, polished and intentional way to guide employers towards seriously considering you as an ideal candidate.

Chapter 2 has covered a wealth of strategies for structuring and formatting your resume content with visual impact, scannability and a cohesive narrative flow. By putting these techniques into practice, you'll be able to construct a truly elevated, best-in-class resume that gets results.

In the next chapter, we'll dive deeper into optimizing your experience sections to showcase accomplishments, transferable skills and quantifiable results that prove your potential value to employers. Continue mastering these structural elements as you prepare to bring your extraordinary credentials to life on the page.

Key Takeaways:
• Strategically choose the ideal resume format (chronological, functional or combination) to best market your background and goals
• Optimize your header with professional contact details and links to establish a polished first impression
• Craft an impactful qualifications summary that hooks employers and previews your unique value proposition
• Determine the most reader-friendly section order and content areas to include based on your strengths
• Incorporate quantified accomplishment statements that tangibly demonstrate the scope of your skills and impact
• Integrate keywords naturally and optimize formatting to ensure your resume is ATS-friendly
• Follow best practices around font choice, spacing, alignment and layout to maximize clarity and scannability
• Leverage visual elements like charts, graphics and diagrams selectively to enhance specific accomplishments
• Thoroughly review for consistency across all formatting, details and to ensure an cohesive, unified narrative

By applying the strategies and techniques covered in this chapter, you can construct a powerfully structured resume that brings your unique career story to life in a polished, visually impactful way.

Your formatting and layout choices will guide the reader's eye intentionally towards your greatest strengths and differentiators. You'll create an extremely clean, professional presentation optimized for both human and machine audiences.

Most importantly, your resume's cohesive narrative flow will thematically market your skills and background as a unified personal brand proposition tailored for your target roles.There will be a clear, compelling through-line that motivates employers to strongly consider you as an ideal candidate to advance in the hiring process.

With the structural foundation now in place, you're ready to dive deeper into the specific strategies for showcasing your experience sections and crafting high-impact accomplishment statements that quantify your potential value.

In the following chapters, you'll master advanced techniques for framing your responsibilities in an achievement-oriented context, highlighting transferable skills for career changers, and promoting the experiences that truly differentiate you from the competition.

Continue practicing intentional formatting, consistent storytelling, and strategic positioning of your credentials as you construct each section. The mastery of structure combined with compelling content is what will allow your extraordinary qualifications to shine.

Chapter 3: Crafting Compelling Experience Sections

With a strong structural foundation and clear understanding of your overarching career narrative in place, it's time to focus on fleshing out your experience sections with rich, compelling detail. This is where you'll bring the full scope of your skills, accomplishments and impact to life through intentional, high-impact storytelling.

In this chapter, you'll learn advanced techniques for framing your responsibilities and achievements in a way that promotes your unique value proposition. You'll master crafting quantified accomplishment statements that tangibly demonstrate the skills and results you can deliver. For career changers, you'll explore strategies to highlight transferable experiences that position you as an ideal candidate for new roles.

Ultimately, the goal is to transform your experience sections from bland, one-dimensional job descriptions into a dynamic, achievement-oriented narrative that markets your potential powerfully. By the end of this chapter, you'll be able to let your extraordinary credentials and "greatest hits" accomplishments truly shine on the page.

Framing Context Effectively

Before diving into your roles and responsibilities, it's critical to establish an appropriate level of context around each experience you're including on your resume. This allows the reader to understand the full scope and environment you were operating within.

For example, when listing your job title, go beyond just the basic name. Provide context around the type of company/organization, industry, team/department you were a part of, number of employees/size, revenue figures, or any other high-level detail that conveys scale and terrain.

You could frame a role like this:

"Managed a 15-person digital marketing team for a $25M e-commerce retailer, overseeing all web, email and paid acquisition channels."

Vs. just listing: "Digital Marketing Manager"

See how that extra context helps the reader envision your experience more fully and understand the stakes? It allows you to position your responsibilities and achievements within an appropriate landscape from the start.

You'll also want to determine how much detail to provide around reporting structure, budget/revenue ownership, geographic scope, and other contextual details based on relevance. For example, a VP of Sales role for a multinational company may want to note regions or territories owned.

The key is to selectively highlight context that allows you to amplify the scope and scale of your experience without overwhelming it with excessive minutiae. Enough detail to create a vivid performance stage for your biggest contributions.

Showcasing Accomplishments with Metrics

With a strong contextual foundation set, the core of your experience sections should focus on showcasing your greatest accomplishments, contributions and results through quantifiable, data-driven achievement statements. This is how you prove your skills in a tangible, credible way.

As a general rule, you'll want to include at least 3-5 bullet points highlighting specific achievements, projects managed, processes improved or challenges overcome for each role. These should be as quantified and number/metrics-driven as possible.

For example, rather than listing responsibilities like:

"Managed email marketing campaigns"

"Collaborated with sales team on lead generation initiatives"

You could reframe those as quantified accomplishments like:

- "Overhauled email marketing campaigns using A/B testing and consumer data segmentation, increasing open rates by 25% and converting $180K in new sales pipeline."
- "Redesigned lead qualification process in partnership with sales team, improving SQL conversion rates by 16% and contributing to 35% YOY revenue growth."

See how those bullet points jump off the page by calling out your skills with hard, measurable data and results? That's what you're aiming for - clear evidence of your ability to drive impact through facts and figures.

Other examples of quantified accomplishment statements:
- "Spearheaded CRM implementation across 17 regional sales centers, increasing data hygiene by 38% and client retention rates by 22%."
- "Managed IT infrastructure overhaul with <2% downtime, ensuring 99.9% network availability and eliminating $275K in annual support costs."
- "Mentored and provided technical leadership to 9 direct reports, delivering code reviews and upskilling to accelerate ramp time by 45%."

As you list out your responsibilities, continually look for opportunities to frame them through a lens of measurable, quantifiable achievements using numbers, metrics, percentages, dollar figures or other hard data points. This is what transforms your experience from vague claims into proven performance.

Crafting High-Impact Accomplishment Bullets

In addition to quantifying your achievements, you'll want to craft accomplishment bullets that are impactful, action-oriented and highlight your unique skills and competencies. The phrasing and vocabulary you use to describe your contributions can make a big difference.

Follow these tips when writing your accomplishment statements:

Lead with Powerful Action Verbs

Don't use bland verbs like "responsible for" or "tasked with." Instead, employ action-packed language that creates momentum and implies your skills in action:

- Spearheaded
- Strategized
- Overhauled
- Optimized
- Revolutionized
- Propelled
- Orchestrated

Use this opportunity to incorporate relevant keywords and hard skills into your phrasing as well. For example:

- "Leveraged machine learning models to forecast demand..."
- "Coded and deployed microservices architecture enabling..."
- "Conducted full-funnel marketing audits to identify gaps..."

Emphasize Your Unique Differentiators

As you're framing accomplishments, make sure to emphasize any experiences or skills that help differentiate your qualifications from other candidates. This allows you to strategically market what makes you distinctly valuable.

For example, if you have a rare technical ability, you may want to emphasize:
"Utilized advanced Python scripting to automate 75% of manual QA processes..."
Or if you have experience in a specialized niche, you could highlight:
"Designed and deployed first-of-its-kind cybersecurity awareness training for 25,000+ employees..."

The bullets that call out your unique strengths and value propositions are what will allow you to truly stand out.

Use Compelling, Vivid Details

Don't just state what you accomplished - use rich descriptive details to bring your achievements to life and create a memorable impression. Paint a vivid picture in the reader's mind by highlighting intriguing aspects like:

• Scope or scale: "...facilitating seamless transition of 250+ global employees"
• Impressive turnaround or transformation: "...repairing and recovering 82% of neglected client relationships"
• Cutting-edge technologies leveraged: "...implementing blockchain traceability for 100% of supply chain data"
• High-stakes, intense environments: "...campaign managing over $25M in annual ad spend across 18 countries"

The more you can weave in compelling specifics and descriptive language, the more your accomplishments will resonate and stick in employers' minds.

Highlight Promotions and Recognition

For applicable roles, be sure to explicitly call out any promotions, stretch opportunities or formal recognition/awards you earned during that experience. Those achievements can help validate the impact and skills you're highlighting.

For example:

• "Promoted to lead developer role after just 6 months, managing a team of 8 engineers."
• "Awarded 'Innovator of the Year' for spearheading a product idea that generated $3M in new revenue."
• "Selected to oversee high-profile international implementation, managing $125K budget and 20% of global user migration."

Touting formal promotions, awards or stretch roles you've earned can lend credibility and social proof to the contributions you're highlighting in your accomplishment statements.

Overall, your goal should be for each experience to contain a series of high-impact, quantified accomplishment bullets that persuasively market your skills through tangible, vivid details. Employers should be able to quickly grasp the full scope of your abilities and potential value through these compelling data points.

Highlighting Transferable Skills for Career Changers

For professionals looking to make a career pivot or transition into a new industry, it's critical to strategically highlight transferable skills and reframe experiences through that new lens. You want to illustrate how your background has prepared you to make an impact in your future roles.

One approach is to group transferable skill accomplishments together into a separate "Relevant Experience" section. This allows you to curate specific achievements that demonstrate your qualifications for your new path without being constrained by chronological order.

For example, as a marketing professional transitioning into a data analyst role, you may have a section like:

Relevant Data Analysis Experience
• Performed in-depth quarterly marketing performance audits across 15 digital channels, analyzing KPIs, identifying trends and developing 32-page data-backed presentations for executive stakeholders.
• Implemented Mixpanel and Amplitude analytics tools to measure user behavior across product funnels, utilizing SQL and data visualization to derive insights for optimization.
• Partnered with data engineers to design and implement Tableau dashboards providing real-time reporting across all digital marketing campaign data for unified measurement.

See how those bullets reframe experiences from a previous career into direct, relevant demonstrations of data analysis abilities? The accomplishments prove applicable technical skills, tools and strategic thinking.

You can then list out your more standard experience chronology in another section, pulling out specific high-impact numbers or transferable accomplishments.

For career changers, it's also useful to incorporate a "Professional Development" or "Certifications" section to highlight any continuing education, bootcamps, online courses or other supplemental training/credentialing you've completed to upskill for your new path.

Additionally, your resume's Summary section is critical for tying all these transferable experiences together into a cohesive high-level narrative around your career transition. You'll want to craft an opening statement that positions you as an intentional candidate making a strategic pivot to a new opportunity.

The key is drawing clear connections for employers to understand how your past has thoroughly prepared you for future impact in your new role or industry. By thoughtfully curating transferable accomplishments and certifications into a unified skills-based story, you can position yourself as a credible, qualified candidate for that transition.

Addressing Employment Gaps or Jumps

For candidates who have any gaps, jumps or unique circumstances in their career chronology, it's important to get ahead of those potential red flags by providing some context and reframing upfront. You'll want to address these instances in a truthful, matter-of-fact way while guiding the narrative to your strengths.

For employment gaps, you could include a simple bullet point listing:

"Took proactive 18-month career break to handle family obligations and personal sabbatical focused on professional development, reskilling and hands-on coding projects."

See how that statement normalizes the gap as an intentional choice and highlights it as a productive period of growth? You can adjust the phrasing based on the specific circumstances, but the key is reframing as a thoughtful decision versus something to be apologetic about.

For jumps between roles, industries or functions, you may want to include a brief transitional note to provide context:

"Pivoted from an accounting role to pursue passion for software development, leveraging transferable data analysis skills and completing a coding bootcamp to ramp up quickly."

This allows you to acknowledge the jump while positioning it as an intentional, prepared career evolution aligned with your interests and motivations.

In general, be upfront about addressing any potential gaps or jumps, but quickly move the narrative toward your strengths, accomplishments and unique qualifications. Don't dwell on the circumstances - focus on the experiences that prove your relevance.

You can also use your resume's Summary section to provide a high-level, forward-looking overview that establishes fit and intentionality around your path. For example:

"Versatile leader with success driving operational excellence across finance, accounting and sales roles. Passionate about leveraging analysis and problem-solving skills to optimize processes and uncover new revenue opportunities."

The key is ensuring your experiences tell a cohesive, intentional story about your journey and the distinct value you can provide to employers.

Promoting Skills that Differentiate You

As you're crafting your experience bullets and accomplishment statements, make sure to strategically emphasize any skills, expertise or achievements that allow you to differentiate yourself and stand out from other candidates.

These could include:

Unique Technical Abilities

If you possess proficiencies in cutting-edge tools, languages or specialties that are highly valuable but not widespread in your field, highlight them prominently. For example:

- "Leveraged pioneering natural language processing techniques to build conversational AI chatbots increasing customer satisfaction rates 35%."
- "Utilized advanced AWS cloud architecture (ECS, Lambda, etc.) to re-platform legacy applications, reducing server costs 68%."

Combining Disparate Skills/Disciplines

Accomplishments where you blend different skills, functions or perspectives in innovative ways can be powerful differentiators. For example:

- "Fusion of UX and neuroscience principles to redesign digital experience increasing mobile conversion rates 29%."
- "Cross-functional project uniting marketing, sales and customer success data to generate unified 360° client intelligence."

Cutting-Edge, Entrepreneurial or Patented Work

If you've driven initiatives that were particularly innovative, entrepreneurial or novel in your company or industry, make sure to emphasize the scope:

- "Co-invented a new proprietary vendor management workflow tool generating $1.2M in operational savings."
- "Spearheaded and launched the startup's first demand generation program, developing a full-funnel marketing engine."

High-Stakes, Intense or Niche Experience

Accomplishments that highlight you thriving in high-stakes, intense or niche environments can help you demonstrate expertise:

- "Oversaw cybersecurity enforcement for 75% of public cloud workloads in hyper-regulated industry."
- "Managed business development and $25M renewals portfolio for Fortune 500 enterprise accounts."

Anytime you have experience that is highly specialized, cutting-edge or simply unique in your field, those accomplishments deserve premium real estate on your resume. Promote the distinct skills and expertise that make you an unparalleled candidate.

You can highlight differentiators through powerful action verbs, vivid details and contextual framing around the scale, scope and complexity of the work. Use your experience section to market what allows you to provide value that other candidates simply cannot match.

Tailoring for Specific Roles and Industries

As you craft your experience section, keep your current career goals and target roles/industries top of mind. You'll want to adjust how you present and prioritize accomplishments based on what will be most relevant and impactful.

For example, if you're pursuing a role in digital marketing, you may want to emphasize skills, tools and results around:

- Paid acquisition and advertising (PPC, retargeting, etc.)
- SEO and content marketing metrics
- A/B testing, conversion funnel optimization
- Marketing automation, campaign management
- Leveraging CRMs and marketing intelligence tools
- Demonstrating quantifiable ROI and revenue impact

Whereas for a project/program management role, you may prioritize accomplishments showcasing skills like:
- Uniting cross-functional teams and managing resources
- Navigating complex environments or regulatory constraints
- Delivering high-stakes initiatives on aggressive timelines
- Implementing new processes, tools or methodologies
- Managing budgets, risk mitigation and stakeholder communications
- Quantifying efficiencies, cost savings or operational impact

You'll want to thoughtfully analyze the core responsibilities and qualifications for your target roles, then strategically highlight the most relevant accomplishments from your experiences that prove those specific skills and capabilities.

Tweak your phrasing, action verbs and quantified details to align with the precise competencies those employers are seeking. Adjust the ordering and depth of bullets accordingly.

You can even repackage accomplishments in different sections (i.e. "Digital Marketing Accomplishments" or "Program/Project Management Experience") to allow you to curate relevant highlights more seamlessly.

The key is tailoring your experience section's focused and narrative to ladder up directly to the unique requirements and priorities for your current career goals and prospecting industries. Conduct the research to deeply understand what will resonate most.

Showcasing Performance Trajectories

For candidates who have spent multiple years with the same company or in the same role, it can be powerful to illustrate your performance trajectory and how you expanded your impact over time. This allows you to showcase professional growth and increasing levels of responsibility.

One approach is to separate out your experience into phases or progression levels within that role, such as:

Hired as Digital Marketing Specialist (2018-2020)
- Accomplishment highlighting initial responsibilities/contributions
- Early successes/promotions earned

Progressed to Digital Marketing Manager (2020-2022)
- Expanded scope managing team of 5 specialists
- Spearheaded new initiatives you owned
- Award/recognition you achieved

Promoted to Senior Digital Marketing Manager (2022-Present)
- Oversee full $5M acquisition budget and department strategy
- Revamped processes and implemented new tools
- Impressive results showcasing current leadership impact

See how that structure demonstrates an upward performance trajectory and increasing ownership over time? You're not just listing a stagnant role, but actively showcasing how you expanded your skills and took on more responsibility.

For roles where you had a bit more consistency in responsibilities over several years, you can illustrate your performance trajectory through the accomplishments themselves by segregating them into chronological phases, for example:

- Initial 2 Years: Highlight accomplishments from getting ramped up, quick wins and process improvements you drove.
- Next 3 Years: Showcase larger programs/initiatives owned, new capabilities/skills developed, increased team leadership.
- Most Recent 1-2 Years: Emphasize biggest, most impressive achievements demonstrating current level of mastery and high impact.

Structuring your experience this way, with a logical narrative arc of growth and progression, can be incredibly powerful for showcasing your performance trajectory to potential employers. It provides a vivid visual storyline of how you've continually expanded your skills and taken on more responsibility over time.

If you have multiple longer tenures at companies, apply this strategy of segregating phases or progression levels for each one. Demonstrate the natural leadership path and increasing impact you've driven consistently across different roles and environments.

For hiring managers, these structured performance trajectory narratives provide concrete evidence that you're a consistent achiever who will continually grow their skills and contributions within new opportunities as well. It's a way to convey your intentional, ongoing pursuit of professional development and mastery.

Framing Accomplishments through a Skills Lens

In addition to structuring your experience sections chronologically, you may also want to consider framing specific accomplishments through a skills-based lens instead. This allows you to curate and elevate achievements that cohesively showcase core competencies.

For example, you could have dedicated sections like:

Marketing Analytics & Data-Driven Strategy

- Leveraged Mixpanel and Amplitude product analytics to identify behavioral cohorts, implementing funnel optimizations increasing activations 35%.
- Developed unified Tableau dashboards consolidating 15+ siloed data sources, automating reporting and surfacing $3M in revenue attribution insights.
- Overhauled UTM tracking and attribution modeling, reducing budget waste by 22% while reallocating towards top-performing channels.

Cross-Functional Leadership & Team Enablement

- Spearheaded implementation of new agile processes uniting product, design and engineering teams, increasing sprint output by 63%.
- Developed and delivered full-scale training curriculum upskilling 120+ employees on CRM and Salesforce best practices, increasing data hygiene 75%.

- Established new growth team structure and operating model, empowering dedicated specialists across acquisition, engagement and monetization.

Presenting your achievements through this skills-based lens allows you to control the narrative and highlight distinct capabilities that may be scattered across different roles or mixed among other responsibilities.

You're able to elevate and consolidate all of the relevant accomplishments that best convey competencies critical for your current goals and target roles. It creates a powerful, thematic showcase of your abilities.

This approach can be especially useful for candidates looking to change roles or industries and needing to illustrate clear transferability of skills from past experiences. It allows you to repackage and reframe your background in a focused, cohesive way that aligns to new opportunities.

You can combine this skills-based framing approach with chronological experience sections, or use it as a standalone way to present your most relevant achievements and differentiators in a high-impact way.

Here are some additional sections to continue rounding out Chapter 3 on crafting compelling experience sections:

Telling Your "Career Narrative" Strategically
While the core of your experience sections should focus on quantified accomplishments and showcasing skills, it's also important to thoughtfully craft an overarching career narrative that connects all of your experiences into a cohesive, forward-looking storyline.

This allows you to explain your "why" and provide context around any transitions, pivots or guiding principles that have shaped your professional journey so far. It's a way to get ahead of potential red flags and reframe your background through an intentional lens aligned with your goals.

For example, your career narrative could focus on themes like:
- Consistent progression into roles with increasing leadership scope and responsibilities
- Intentional skills-broadening by taking on cross-functional or "catalyst" roles
- Personal interests or values that have motivated you to pivot industries/disciplines
- An entrepreneurial mindset driving you to seek out new challenges and innovations
- Transferring your expertise into a new domain to tackle more complex problems

You can weave this career narrative throughout your experience section by:
- Crafting a concise "Role Overview" opening line that frames the high-level context and priorities for that experience through your narrative lens.
- Sprinkling in transitional bullets that provide insight into the "why" behind any pivots, promotions or role changes.
- Highlighting accomplishments that exemplify key themes or mindsets from your narrative (i.e. leadership trajectory, entrepreneurial approach, technical depth, etc.)

For example:
"Driven by an entrepreneurial passion for envisioning and launching new go-to-market initiatives, I joined Acme Corp to help establish the company's first dedicated demand generation function."

Or

"After establishing a proven track record of operational excellence and continuous improvement, I purposefully transitioned into a role uniting cross-functional IT and engineering teams to drive larger-scale technology transformation."

By artfully crafting an authentic career narrative, you provide valuable context around your journey that hiring managers may not get solely from reading your chronological experience. You shape the story proactively and differentiate yourself as an intentional, self-aware professional.

This narrative through-line should ladder up to Marketing your unique value proposition and making a strong case for why you're an ideal candidate for the types of roles you're now pursuing. It allows you to control the messaging around your background and reframe any potential obstacles as thoughtful, purposeful evolutions.

Quantifying the 'Soft' Skills

While the emphasis of your experience sections should skew towards quantifiable accomplishments, it's also important to demonstrate mastery of critical soft skills like leadership, communication, strategic thinking and other intangible competencies.

While these can be trickier to capture with hard numbers, you can still thoughtfully weave quantified data points throughout to validate your capabilities:

Leadership & People Management
- Awarded "Top Manager" recognition after driving 82% YOY increase in employee engagement scores
- Established new Learning & Development function, launching training programs contributing to 27% faster ramp times for new hires
- Mentored and provided professional development to 15 direct reports, with 65% being promoted within 18 months

Strategic Planning & Execution
- Developed and presented go-to-market strategy to executive team, securing $25M funding for initiative implementation
- Spearheaded 3-year strategic plan, defining product roadmap and growth targets contributing to successful $85M acquisition
- Overhauled territory planning using data-driven modeling, optimizing coverage and increasing renewals by $12M

Communication & Stakeholder Engagement
- Facilitated 50+ presentations and workshops educating 500 partners on new product positioning and value proposition
- Established quarterly business review program, presenting KPI progress to CEO and Board of Directors

- Authored communications strategy securing buy-in across 7 regional teams for ERP implementation affecting 8,000 employees

Look for opportunities to quantify things like:
- Scope or scale (team size, stakeholders, budget/revenue oversight, etc.)
- Operational impact (efficiency gains, cost savings, process improvements)
- Reach or influence (number of people/teams engaged, served, etc.)
- Rates and percentages (turnover, satisfaction, adoption, etc.)

Any numbers, metrics or data points you can provide give credible evidence of your mastery in areas like leadership, strategy and communication. They help validate your skills beyond just responsibilities.

Ultimately, your experience sections should showcase a well-rounded blend of quantifiable hard skills and measurable "soft" proficiencies.

Promoting Your "Career Mastery"

For candidates with significant experience or lengthy tenures in particular roles, it can be powerful to establish a cohesive narrative around your "career mastery" in that core area of expertise. This allows you to position yourself as a veritable subject matter expert and "go-to" authority.

The key is using your experience section to build a multi-dimensional profile that showcases the full breadth and depth of your capabilities in that focused domain over time. You'll want to highlight accomplishments and skills that ladder up to establishing your credibility and progressive mastery.

For example, for a marketing leader looking to promote their expertise, you could segregate sections like:

Marketing Strategy & Vision Casting

• Developed and presented a 3-year integrated marketing strategy to the executive team, securing a $35M annual budget to execute...

• Overhauled brand messaging and value proposition, increasing consideration rates by 37% and contributing to $25M ARR growth...

• Established new marketing operations function, implementing enablement tools and processes embraced by 200+ global teams...

Campaign Development & Execution Mastery

• Generated $185M in pipeline from performance marketing initiatives leveraging advanced analytics and multivariate testing...

• Pioneered account-based marketing pilot achieving 45% higher SDR conversion rates and $8.2M in new enterprise business...

• Scaled always-on nurture campaigns globally, improving MQL volumes 68% while maintaining strict quality thresholds...

Marketing Technology Expertise

• Spearheaded implementation of Marketo, consolidating 14 disconnected systems and creating unified lead management database...

• Deployed Optimizely platform and built experimentation practice, generating $12M from winning campaign variants in first year...

• Pioneered AI deployment via integration with Einstein & Bright scoring, increasing MQL conversion rates 35%...

See how those section buckets combine to create a unified, multifaceted narrative positioning you as a full-fledged marketing master? You're providing evidence of your progressive expertise in everything from high-level strategy to hands-on execution to technical mastery.

Another approach could be to layer in a chronological aspect showcasing how your mastery evolved over time:

Marketing Manager (2016-2018): Early accomplishments highlighting core skills development

Senior Marketing Manager (2018-2020): Progression into managing teams and scaling responsibilities

Director of Marketing (2020-Present): Current scope and full breadth of mastery showcased

You could even combine those techniques by segregating role-based sections into subsections showcasing the chronological progression of mastery within each categorical area.

The key is thoughtfully curating and packaging your most impressive accomplishments and skills in a way that creates a cohesive, authoritative narrative around your subject matter expertise.

Employers should be able to walk away with a clear, credible understanding of the rare level of mastery you possess in that particular domain based on the cumulative evidence provided. You're not just highlighting skills - you're building an air-tight case to be considered a true master in your field.

Telling a Human Story

While the core of your experience section should be focused on quantifiable data that proves your skills and abilities, it's also important to avoid making your content read as overly mechanical or robotic. Injecting some personal narrative elements can help reinforce your unique voice and create a more authentic, human connection with the reader.

One approach is to incorporate brief personal storylines or backstories that provide context around pivotal career moments or particularly impactful accomplishments. For example:

"My passion for environmentalism began after attending a lecture on sustainable agriculture during college. This inspired me to join a nonprofit urban farming cooperative, where I overhauled processes and technology resulting in a 40% increase in crop yields..."

See how that translates an accomplishment into more of a personal origin story? It humanizes your experience while reinforcing your motivations and values.

You could also share inspirational anecdotes or challenges overcome:

"After a difficult 9-month stretch of project delays and vendor failures, I took it upon myself to get certified in agile methodologies and change management practices. This allowed me to get the $25M initiative back on track through a new delivery framework embraced by all stakeholders..."

These types of personal storylines provide a window into your emotional intelligence, growth mindset and ability to persevere through adversity. They make your accomplishments feel more hard-won and impactful.

Here are some additional ways to inject more personal narrative elements and human storytelling into your experience sections:

Showcase Your Distinctive Voice and Personality
While maintaining an overall professional tone, look for opportunities to let your authentic voice and personality shine through in your phrasing and descriptive language. This will help make your accomplishments feel more genuine and

For example, rather than a dry bullet like:
"Optimized website load times 37% by implementing accelerated mobile page coding"
You could showcase more voice with a statement like:

"Transformed our mobile e-commerce site from a sluggish nightmare into a zippy, conversion-humming dream by implementing accelerated mobile page coding - shaving load times by 37% and boosting sales $1.2M."

See how that second version paints a richer, more engaging picture while still providing the key technical details? The descriptive flair and humor help make the accomplishment stand out.

You can get creative with analogies, metaphors, or even injecting some light sarcasm or wittiness when appropriate for your personal brand. Just don't go over-the-top; a few splashes of distinctive personality here and there will make your content far more engaging and human.

Share Glimpses into Your Motivations and Values
As you're describing key accomplishments, look for natural opportunities to weave in anecdotes or insights that provide a window into your core motivations, priorities and values as a professional.

For example:

"As a firm believer that customer experience is the true heart of any business, I spearheaded an overhaul of our support processes, reducing response times 67% and boosting retention rates 23%."

Or

"Deeply committed to empowering my team's professional growth, I established biweekly coaching sessions and learning workshops, resulting in a 43% increase in direct reports earning promotions."

These types of glimpses allow employers to better understand what drives and fulfills you beyond just technical skills. They provide a more multidimensional view of you as a human being and employee.

Convey Passion and Enthusiasm

Don't be afraid to let your excitement and enthusiasm for your work shine through in your phrasing. Employers want to hire people who will be energized and passionate contributors.

You could describe an accomplishment like:
"After being blown away by the power of predictive analytics, I became obsessed with exploring how we could apply advanced machine learning models within our marketing programs..."

Or

"I've always been endlessly fascinated by the intersection of design and human behavior, so the opportunity to revolutionize our user experience through an innovative neuromarketing approach was an absolute thrill..."

Peppering in these types of passionate reflections and personal anecdotes can be incredibly powerful for allowing your human energy and authenticity to radiate.

Ultimately, the goal is to strike a balance between quantifiable data and accomplishments that demonstrate your hard skills with these types of personal narrative touches that give a glimpse into you as a human being. You want employers to walk away with a clear picture of both your technical abilities and the unique motivations and personality you'd bring to their organization.

So don't be afraid to strategically loosen the reins and inject some distinctive personal flair into your experience sections. Just be sure to maintain an overall professional, achievement-oriented approach. With the right blend of data and personal narrative, your resume will resonate on a deeper human level.

Key Takeaways:
• Provide context around scope, scale and environment to effectively frame each role's responsibilities and accomplishments
• Quantify achievements through numbers, metrics, data and tangible results to prove capabilities
• Craft high-impact bullet points using powerful action verbs and vivid details to elevate accomplishments
• Highlight skills and experiences that differentiate you as a uniquely qualified candidate
• Reframe and repackage experiences through a transferable skills lens for career changers
• Address employment gaps or transitions proactively while quickly pivoting to showcase strengths
• Promote specialties and experiences that position you as a master of your core domain
• Illustrate performance trajectories and increasing responsibilities over time within roles
• Tailor accomplishments and highlight most relevant skills based on current goals
• Inject personal narrative elements like backstories and glimpses into motivations/values

By implementing the strategies covered in this chapter, you can transform your experience sections from flat, one-dimensional job descriptions into a dynamic, high-impact marketing narrative that persuasively showcases your potential value to employers.

Your roles and accomplishments will be framed through vivid, quantified detail that allows employers to vividly contextualize the skills and capabilities you bring to the table. The way you've packaged and promoted your credentials will powerfully support your overall career narrative and unique value proposition.

At the same time, you'll have infused these sections with personal narrative touches that provide a window into your authentic motivations, values and distinct way of showing up as a professional. You'll make your achievements feel more genuine and resonant by allowing your human energy to shine through.

The experience section is arguably the most critical component of your resume. It's where you have the opportunity to bring the full scope of your skills, results and potential impact to life through intentional, high-impact storytelling.

By applying the comprehensive techniques in this chapter, you'll be able to craft an extraordinary experience section that leaves employers utterly compelled by your qualifications and excited to learn more about you as a candidate.

The strategies you've learned allow you to control the narrative, promote your greatest strengths, establish credibility and differentiate yourself from the competition - all through the lens of your defined personal brand.

With your experience sections fully fleshed out in a compelling way, you're now equipped to elevate the remaining components of your resume to create a cohesive, best-in-class marketing portfolio for your career ambitions.

The journey of resume mastery continues with highlighting additional skills, education and credentials that ladder up to your unique value proposition. Keep practicing intentional, achievement-oriented storytelling as you construct each section. Your extraordinary qualifications are ready to truly shine!

Chapter 4: Enhancing With Additional Sections

While your experience bullets are the core of your resume, thoughtfully highlighting additional credentials and skills through targeted sections can elevate your marketing portfolio to new levels. These components allow you to expand on specialized areas of expertise and paint a more comprehensive professional portrait.

In this chapter, you'll master strategies for showcasing your academic pedigree, certifications, technical skills and extracurricular achievements in an impactful way. You'll learn to determine which additional credentials are most relevant for promoting your unique value proposition based on your current goals.

By rounding out your qualifications through a strategic mix of additional sections, you control the narrative and highlight the full breadth of assets that make you an ideal candidate for the roles you're pursuing. You establish a multidimensional professional brand that extends beyond just your work experience.

Formatting the Education & Credentials Sections

For many roles, particularly early or mid-career, your formal education and any relevant certifications or training deserve their own dedicated sections on your resume. These components can influence how employers perceive your qualifications and potential.

When listing your academic credentials, be sure to include:
- Full degree name/title and field of study (i.e. Bachelor of Science in Marketing)
- Academic institution's name
- Attendance years (or graduation year if within last 10 years)
- Location of institution
- GPA (if 3.5 or above from a respected university)
- Academic honors like Latin distinctions, Dean's List, etc.

You can optionally include relevant coursework, academic projects, research experience or other accomplishments that showcase applicable skills or reinforce your fit for particular roles.

For example, as a STEM student you may want to highlight any technical electives, coding courses or independent research publications. As a business student, you could feature any entrepreneurial projects, case competitions or consulting experience.

Format all of your education entries consistently using clear titles, locations, date ordering and ample white spacing between each listing. If you have multiple degrees, lead with your highest level of academic achievement first (i.e. list a master's before a bachelor's).

For certifications, licenses or professional development programs, you'll generally want to format these in their own distinct section separate from formal education. Include the full certification name, issuing organization, date completed and any other qualifying credentials like expiration dates or ID numbers.

Some examples:

Project Management Professional (PMP) - Project Management Institute (2019 - Present)

Certified Information Systems Security Professional (CISSP) - ISC2 (Cert #123456 - Exp. 2025)

Google Analytics Certified Professional - Google (Credential ID: GA-012345)

As with education, be sure to include any certifications that are particularly relevant and impressive for the roles you're targeting. Prioritize them accordingly and consider including a brief description if the credential's name alone doesn't indicate its significance.

Between your educational background and any prestigious certifications, these components can significantly elevate your credibility and perceived qualifications. Use dedicated sections to showcase them prominently.

Highlighting Your Technical Skills Portfolio

In many industries and roles, your specific technical skills and proficiencies are as paramount as experience itself. Dedicated sections highlighting your relevant hard skills can be powerful resume differentiators.

Typical technical skills categories to include sections for:
- Programming Languages (Python, Java, C++, etc.)
- Software & Tools (Salesforce, Tableau, Figma, etc.)
- Data & Analytics (SQL, Hadoop, Machine Learning, etc.)
- IT & Systems (AWS, Networking, Cybersecurity, etc.)
- Design & Creative (Adobe Creative Suite, UX/UI, etc.)

For each category, be sure to include your specific skills and versions/levels of expertise where applicable. You can use formatting like:

Python (5 years): Pandas, NumPy, scikit-learn, Django
SQL (8 years): MySQL, PostgreSQL, Microsoft SQL Server, Redshift
Salesforce (3 years): Sales Cloud, Service Cloud, Marketing Cloud, Pardot

This allows you to promote a robust technical skills portfolio in a clean, scannable way while providing more detail than just a vague list.

You can optionally incorporate icons, logos or visual elements to make specific technical skills pop off the page. This can be especially powerful for design, UX or creative roles where visuals could enhance your credibility.

Showcasing Certifications and Professional Development

For many fields, highlighting relevant certifications, licenses and professional development programs can be critical for demonstrating up-to-date expertise and a commitment to continuous learning. Employers want to see you've invested in keeping your skills sharp.

When listing certifications, be sure to include:

• The full name/title of the certification

• The offering institution, organization or company

• The year(s) obtained and/or expiration dates

• Any ID numbers or credentials associated with it

• A brief description if the certification name isn't self-explanatory

For example:

Project Management Professional (PMP) - Project Management Institute (2019 - Present)

Certified Information Systems Security Professional (CISSP) - (ISC)² - (Cert #123456 - Exp. 2025)

Google Analytics Certified Professional - Google (Credential ID: GA-012345)

Format these certifications consistently, either in their own dedicated section or as part of a combined "Credentials" section alongside your formal education.

For particularly impressive or rigorous certifications, you can elevate them by incorporating:

• Badges or logos associated with the credentialing organization

• Percentile rankings (i.e. "Scored in the top 15th percentile")

• Descriptions of the skills mastered or assessed

• Projects or work samples that exemplify the applied capabilities

The key is positioning these certifications as substantive endorsements of your qualifications from respected third-party institutions and industry authorities.

Similarly for professional development programs like executive education, coding bootcamps or corporate training, be sure to list:

• The full program name and/or curriculum focus

• The offering institution, company or organization

• Year(s) attended and any credentials or certificates earned

• Specific skills, tools or concepts covered

For example:

Data Science Immersive | Certificate in Data Analytics - BrainStation (2022)

- Curriculum: Python, SQL, machine learning, Tableau, experimental design

Wharton Executive Education | Business Analytics Program - University of Pennsylvania (2021)
- Completed coursework in data modeling, visualization, Hadoop, forecasting

Listing out these professional development programs showcases your commitment to continuous upskilling and growth. It validates your evolving skill sets beyond just work experience.

Ultimately, these certification and professional development sections establish you as a dedicated lifelong learner committed to maintaining cutting-edge expertise. They provide third-party endorsements of your qualifications from respected institutions and organizations.

Highlighting Extracurriculars and Memberships

In addition to core technical skills and credentials, extracurricular activities, volunteer experiences and professional memberships can be valuable resume line items for rounding out your qualifications and adding some personal dimension.

For activities and volunteer roles, be sure to include:
- The name of the organization, club or initiative
- Your title, role or responsibilities
- The date range of your involvement
- Any accomplishments, contributions or impacts

For example:

Habitat for Humanity

Volunteer Construction Crew Lead (2020 - Present)
- Coordinated 25+ volunteers to build affordable eco-friendly housing for 10 families
- Managed site logistics, scheduling, materials and safety protocols

University Data Science Club
Co-Founder & President (2017 - 2019)
- Grew membership to 65+ students across STEM majors
- Organized coding competitions, tutorials and guest speaker events

These types of experiences showcase skills in leadership, project management, communication and initiative. They provide a window into your interests, values and commitment to larger causes.

Similarly for professional associations and memberships, be sure to list:
- The full name of the organization
- Your membership level or credentials
- Date range you've been involved
- Any notable roles, contributions or achievements

For example:
American Marketing Association (AMA)
- Professional Certified Marketer (2020 - Present)
- Seattle Chapter: Served as Director of Communications (2018-2020)

IEEE Computer Society
- Student Member (2016 - 2018)
- Cybersecurity Community: Organizing Committee Member

Including these types of affiliations showcases your connection to larger professional communities and commitment to upholding industry standards and best practices.
While these may seem like smaller supplemental sections, they provide important personal context and differentiators.

Incorporating Other Achievement Sections

Depending on your background and accomplishments, there may be other unique sections you'll want to incorporate onto your resume to fully showcase the breadth of your skills and qualifications.

Some potential additional sections to consider:

Awards & Honors

Use this section to highlight any notable awards, distinctions or recognition you've received throughout your career or education. Format entries like:
- "Employee of the Year" - Company Name (2021)
- Awarded "Top Selling Sales Rep" - 3 consecutive years
- Dean's List - 6 semesters, Oklahoma State University

Publications & Speaking

If you've published articles, research papers, blogs or books related to your field, include them in this section with details like:
- "Optimizing Cloud Security in Highly Regulated Industries" - Published in Network World (2022)
- Cybersecurity Blog - 25,000+ Subscribers (https://cybersecblog.com)
- "Mastering React" (ebook) - Published on Amazon (2020)

You can also include any professional conferences, panels or guest lectures you've spoken at in this section.

Languages

For roles that require multilingual skills, create a subsection listing your languages and proficiency levels. You can use categories like:
- English (Native Proficiency)
- Spanish (Full Professional Proficiency)
- French (Limited Working Proficiency)

Projects & Portfolios

If you have notable projects, coding samples, design work or portfolios that showcase hands-on skills and capabilities, you may want a dedicated section including:

• Title/name of the project

• Short 1-2 sentence description of the project

• Links, documentation or samples to view the work

Be selective about only including projects that are highly relevant and impressive for your current career goals.

Military Experience

For veterans, be sure to include your military experience and any relevant skills, training or accomplishments like:

• U.S. Marine Corps (2005 - 2011)

• Sergeant, Infantry

• Expertise: Leadership, logistics, risk mitigation

The key for any additional sections is to make judicious decisions around what accomplishments, skills and credentials are most impactful to include based on your current career trajectory. Use them to strategically fill out your qualifications.

Don't go overboard trying to include every single achievement or experience. Prioritize quality over quantity and focus on highlighting the most differentiating and relevant credentials that ladder back up to your core value proposition.

When done with intention, these additional sections can elevate your resume from a one-dimensional work history into a rich, multifaceted marketing portfolio that showcases the full depth of your professional brand.

Here are some additional tips for enhancing your resume with other sections and formatting elements:

Leveraging Visuals and Multimedia

While the core of your resume should remain text-focused for scannability, you can selectively incorporate some visual elements to add polish and reinforce your unique brand. Use them strategically to differentiate your skills and accomplishments.

Data Visualizations

If you have expertise in areas like data analysis, business intelligence or marketing analytics, include samples of dashboards, reports or data visualizations you've created. This provides credible evidence of your technical abilities.

Design Portfolios

For roles in creative fields like UX/UI, graphic design or marketing, embed samples of your portfolio work to showcase your skills visually. Use compact images, thumbnails or links.

Technical Diagrams

For more technical roles, you can include simplified workflow diagrams, system architecture or process maps you've created as visuals to illustrate your work.

Skills Logos and Iconography

To make your technical skills sections jump off the page, incorporate simple brand logos or icons to represent each competency. This formatting can increase scannability.

Multimedia and Interactive Content

If appropriate for your field, you can embed multimedia samples like video reels, podcasts, websites or interactive content to showcase your abilities in those mediums.

When incorporating visuals, balance is key. Your resume shouldn't become a distracting showpiece - the writing should still be the primary focus. Use visuals judiciously as supportive evidence highlighting specific skills or achievements.

Formatting for Digital Resumes

While traditional PDF or Word resumes are still standard, more employers are also accepting online, digital or multimedia resume formats. If submitting this way, you can get more creative with interactive elements like:

- Embedded hyperlinks to samples, portfolios or multimedia content
- Expandable sections that allow viewers to toggle additional details
- Animated graphics, motion design or dynamic data visualizations
- Video, audio or multimedia introductions and headers
- Navigation menus and internal document links for improved UX

These interactive elements can make your digital resume more engaging while aligning with your personal brand. For example, a UX designer could incorporate site-mapping and mobile responsiveness into their resume layout

.

However, be thoughtful about using these enhancements consistently and avoiding gimmicky effects that could come across as distracting. Make sure your digital formatting aligns with the companies and roles you're targeting.

Additionally, you'll want to optimize any digital resumes for accessibility by using best practices around text sizes, color contrasts and navigation for viewers across different devices.

Leveraging Testimonials and Third-Party Validation
For roles in client-facing fields like consulting, sales or services, you can create additional impact by incorporating quotes, testimonials or other third-party validation that highlights your reputation and credibility.

For example, you could include brief testimonial excerpts like:
"[Candidate] is an exceptional strategic partner who consistently drives impact. Their work on our digital transformation project resulted in over $2M in cost savings."
- Jane Doe, SVP of Operations, Acme Corporation

"One of the most knowledgeable and passionate marketing minds I've worked with. [Candidate's] creative approach to our rebrand generated double-digit increases in brand sentiment across all channels."

- John Doe, Chief Marketing Officer, Beta Inc.

These types of succinct, results-driven testimonials from reputable clients or colleagues provide powerful social proof of your skills and value. They validate your accomplishments through the lens of others.

You can also include any prestigious awards, press mentions or credentials that provide third-party endorsement of your expertise and impact.

For example:
• Featured in Forbes' "30 Under 30" in Marketing & Advertising (2022)
• Recognized as "Agency Innovator of the Year" - AdWeek (2021)
• Member: Exclusive Invitation-Only Mastermind Group for Blockchain Leaders

These inclusions establish your credibility and influence within your professional community. They position you as a respected, sought-after expert in your field.

When incorporating third-party validation, focus on quality over quantity. A few high-impact, concise endorsements or credentials will be more impressive than listing numerous unremarkable ones.

The key is using these elements to reinforce your unique value proposition and substantiate the strengths you've been promoting throughout your resume. They provide social proof and credibility to elevate your personal brand.

Key Takeaways:
• Dedicate sections to highlight your academic pedigree, including degrees, institutions, GPAs and honors

- Showcase relevant certifications, licenses and professional development programs to validate current expertise
- Create technical skills sections that provide robust portfolios of your software, tools and programming abilities
- Incorporate extracurricular activities, volunteering and professional memberships that demonstrate initiative and dimension
- Consider additional sections for awards, publications, language proficiencies and relevant projects/portfolios
- Use visuals like charts, diagrams and samples judiciously to support and differentiate specific skills
- Optimize for digital formats by embedding multimedia, interactive elements and tailoring UX/layouts
- Leverage third-party validation through quotes, testimonials and credentials to reinforce credibility

By thoughtfully incorporating additional sections beyond just your work experience, you create a rich, multidimensional marketing portfolio that highlights the full breadth of your professional capabilities.

Your academic achievements, certifications and technical skills provide concrete evidence and endorsement of your qualifications. Your extracurricular interests, community involvement and outside accomplishments showcase initiative and personal dimension.

Any relevant visuals, portfolios and multimedia samples provide impactful proof points that clearly illustrate your skills in action. And third-party testimonials or credentials lend social proof and credibility to the strengths you're promoting.

Combined, these additional sections elevate you from just a collection of work experiences into a comprehensive, multifaceted personal brand proposition. You control the full narrative and highlight what makes you a uniquely qualified, well-rounded professional.

As you've learned, the key is curation and prioritization. Don't just include every possible credential or accomplishment. Be highly judicious about only incorporating additional sections and elements that are directly relevant to your current career goals and the roles you're targeting.

Everything should tie back to reinforcing your core value proposition through the lens of your defined personal brand. You want to create a cohesive, thematic presentation that markets you as an ideal candidate for the opportunities you're pursuing.

With the techniques from this chapter, you now can construct a rich, compelling qualifications portfolio that extends far beyond just listing your work experience. You control the full narrative and spotlight all of the impressive skills and achievements that make you stand out.

The journey of resume mastery is about intentionally shaping how your entire background and unique combination of credentials is positioned. By enhancing your resume with strategically curated additional sections, you propel your extraordinary qualifications to new levels of marketing impact.

Get ready to integrate these concepts as you put the final polish on your personal branding masterpiece! Your unified, best-in-class resume portfolio is taking shape.

Chapter 5: Polishing and Perfecting Your Resume

You've defined your authentic career narrative and personal brand pillars. You've structured and formatted your content in a visually compelling, reader-friendly way. You've filled out your experience sections with quantified accomplishments that prove your skills. And you've enhanced your qualifications portfolio with additional prestigious credentials.

Now it's time to apply the final polish to ensure your extraordinary resume is a flawless, cohesive masterpiece that will make a powerful impression on employers. Even minor inconsistencies or errors can undermine your credibility, so we'll explore strategies for perfecting every element.

In this chapter, you'll master the nuances of finessing your phrasing and fine-tuning details with an editor's eye. You'll learn to thoughtfully adapt content for different career opportunities while maintaining your authentic personal brand voice. And you'll develop a keen eye for identifying and resolving any potential red flags or gaps in your narrative.

By completing this polishing process, you'll ensure your resume resonates with utmost professionalism, intentionality and impact. You'll be able to confidently share your extraordinary qualifications with employers and move forward in the hiring process with poise. The mastery of perfecting your materials is the final step to unlocking your career success.

Reviewing For Consistency Across All Elements

Now that you've constructed comprehensive sections showcasing your background and accomplishments, the first crucial polishing step is to thoroughly cross-check every element of your resume for consistency. Even minor discrepancies in formatting, dates, titles or other details can raise red flags and undermine your credibility with employers. With a critical eye, carefully review and cross-reference items like:

- Formatting styles (font sizes, bold/italics, spacing, alignment, etc.)
- Date ranges listed for each role or accomplishment
- Spelling of company names, locations, project titles, etc.
- Verb tenses used for current vs. past experiences
- Personal pronouns (consistent use of "I" vs. third person)
- Your name/header details listed consistently on each page
- Numeric formatting for numbers, currency, percentages, etc.

As you're reviewing, be on the lookout for any contradictory information or gaps that could raise eyebrows. For example, if you list skills or accomplishments that don't seem aligned with the responsibilities of a particular role, be prepared to clarify or reframe those components.

It can also be helpful to create a separate "Global Terms" document logging consistent terminology, acronyms, titles or other details you'll reference repeatedly throughout your materials. This ensures you're using the same verbiage each time for maximum consistency.

Remember, employers will be scrutinizing your resume closely for any potential inaccuracies or inconsistencies. By taking the time to thoroughly cross-check every element with an editor's eye, you demonstrate your utmost polish, attention to detail and credibility as a candidate.

Tailoring Content For Specific Opportunities

While your core qualifications and personal brand pillars should remain consistent, it's important to tailor certain components of your resume for specific roles and companies you're actively pursuing. This allows you to optimize relevance and highlight different aspects of your background strategically.

As you prepare to apply for a particular opportunity, take some time to analyze the job description, research the company's culture/values, and identify the key qualifications and skills required. Then, carefully review your existing resume content through that tailored lens.

You may choose to make adjustments like:
• Updating your high-level resume summary to incorporate relevant keywords from the job posting
• Shuffling the order of your experience bullets to elevate the most applicable accomplishments
• Modifying your technical skills lists to spotlight the exact tools and proficiencies they're seeking
• Incorporating specific details, metrics or project examples that directly demonstrate the qualifications

For example, while your core marketing background may be consistent, you could tweak components for:
• A content marketing role at a B2B SaaS company (emphasize skills like SEO, sales enablement, ABM)
• A performance marketing position at a D2C ecommerce brand (prioritize paid acquisition, funnel optimization)
• A marketing operations role at a large enterprise (highlight marketing automation, CRM implementation)

The key is identifying the precise competencies each specific role prioritizes and customizing how you frame and package your relevant experiences accordingly.

This tailoring process helps ensure your resume speaks the same "language" as the job descriptions and aligns perfectly with what that particular company is looking for.

Optimizing Keyword Integration

In today's hiring landscape where recruiters use applicant tracking systems (ATS) to screen resumes, strategically integrating relevant keywords is critical. You want to ensure your content gets through those initial filters and into human hands.

As you prepare to apply for specific roles, take some time to analyze the job descriptions and research common skill/qualification keywords for that type of position and industry. Make a list of the frequently recurring nouns and phrases.

Then, carefully review all sections of your resume to seamlessly integrate those target keywords in context throughout your content. Look for opportunities to:
• Swap out synonymous terms you're already using for the prioritized keywords
• Incorporate acronyms or industry jargon that demonstrates fluency
• Reframe accomplishments to naturally include key tools, skills or concepts
• Adjust your core skills/proficiencies lists to align with requirements

For example, a job posting for a data scientist role may emphasize skills like:
Python, SQL, machine learning, Spark, Hadoop, scikit-learn, TensorFlow, data modeling, A/B testing

You'd want to ensure phrases and terms like those are prominently integrated throughout your experience bullets, accomplishments, skills sections and any other applicable areas.

The key is maintaining a natural, readable flow in your writing rather than just stuffing keywords arbitrarily. Use them in the proper context to demonstrate relevance. Strategically emphasize the keywords that convey your qualifications.

You'll also want to be smart about keyword density and repetition. Aim to strike a balance by integrating high-priority keywords 5-7 times in diverse sections without going overboard. Sprinkle in secondary keywords more moderately.

With thoughtful keyword optimization, your resume will be sure to catch the eye of both ATS filters and human recruiters/hiring managers who are attuned to those target terms. You'll come across as a precise fit for the role's requirements.

Addressing Potential Gaps or Red Flags

Even with a stellar resume crafted around your strongest qualifications, you may have some potential gaps or red flags in your background that could raise questions for employers. It's important to get ahead of those issues and address them proactively.

Some common potential gaps or red flags could include:
- Extended periods of unemployment between roles
- Frequent job changes or "job hopping" over a short period
- Lack of direct experience related to the roles you're pursuing
- Incomplete, missing or irregular date ranges for certain roles
- Transitioning between vastly different roles, industries or functions

Rather than leaving those gaps open to interpretation or assumption, directly acknowledge them in a brief, matter-of-fact way that reframes the situation positively.

For example:

Employment Gap:
"Took an intended 18-month career break to handle family obligations and personal passion projects in 2019-2020."

Frequent Job Changes:
"Gained experience across multiple high-growth startups and fast-paced environments between 2017-2019 before seeking a long-term fit."

Lack of Direct Experience:
"While my background is in [previous role], my transferable skills in [relevant skills] and passion for [new industry] make me an ideal candidate."

The key is to address the potential red flag head-on in 1-2 concise, honest sentences that put it into positive context. Explain it matter-of-factly, then quickly pivot to highlighting your strengths, intentions and unique value proposition.

You can choose to incorporate these gap/red flag statements directly into your experience section bullets, summary statement, cover letter or as a separate brief note on your resume. The goal is to get ahead of the issue and reframe it through a refreshing lens of transparency.

By addressing potential gaps or concerns proactively, you demonstrate self-awareness and take control of the narrative before employers can make negative assumptions. You position yourself as a thoughtful professional, not someone with something to hide.
This simple acknowledgment allows you to steer the conversation around any issues from the start. You're able to quickly pivot towards showcasing how your extraordinary qualifications outweigh any potential concerns.

Promoting Your Unique Differentiators

As you apply the final polish, make sure you're intentionally promoting what allows you to stand out from other candidates. Highlight the unique skills, experiences and qualifications that differentiate you as an ideal fit.

Some ways to make your differentiators shine:

In Your Summary/Opening

Use the prime real estate of your opening summary statement to immediately capture attention around what makes you distinctly qualified. You could open with a high-impact statement like:

"Innovative leader combining X and Y expertise to deliver Z..."
"Multi-disciplinary background uniting A, B and C capabilities..."

Within Experience Bullets

As you're highlighting key accomplishments, emphasize any that allowed you to showcase rare technical abilities, blended disciplines, or cutting-edge/entrepreneurial approaches.

For example:
- "Pioneered use of machine learning for demand forecasting, increasing forecast accuracy by 35%."
- "Cross-leveraged data science and UX research to redesign customer analytics platform, reducing churn 18%."

Dedicated "Differentiators" Section

You can even create a dedicated section clearly spelling out what allows you to provide unique value. For example:

"Differentiating Expertise:
- 10+ years experience in highly-regulated FinTech/Blockchain space
- Proficient developing on Ethereum, Hyperledger and Corda blockchain frameworks
- Unique multidisciplinary background combining finance, computer science and legal"

Technical Skills Callouts

In your skills sections, consider using visual callouts or indicators to make any rare, advanced or niche technical skills jump off the page. You can use annotations, icons, etc.

The key is using multiple tactics to clearly convey what allows you to stand out and deliver distinct values that other candidates cannot match. Make your unique differentiators unmissable.

Establishing Your Personal Brand Voice

At this stage, it's also important to ensure your resume materials authentically capture your unique personal brand voice and personality. You want your extraordinary qualifications to be presented in a way that resonates with your genuine professional persona.

As you're reviewing your content, make adjustments to fine-tune phrasing and language to align with your personal brand attributes like:
- Communication and writing style (i.e. concise, direct or more descriptive)
- Levels of formality vs. conversational tone
- Humility and confidence levels when promoting accomplishments
- Injections of passion, humor or distinctive flair where appropriate

For example, a more technical brand voice may use crisper language like:
"Developed and deployed microservices using AWS Lambda and ECS, reducing server overhead 43%."

Versus a brand voice highlighting more creativity:
"Revolutionized archaic monolithic architecture by implementing sleek, serverless microservices leveraging AWS Lambda and ECS - decimating overhead costs by 43%."

There's no right or wrong voice - it should feel authentic to how you naturally describe your work. If your materials come across as stiff or embellished in a way that doesn't align with your true persona, edit them to better capture your sincere brand voice.

You can even incorporate short personal anecdotes or insights that provide a glimpse into your motivations, values and personality. Just be sure to maintain an overall professional, achievement-oriented tone.

Ultimately, the goal is to produce a cohesive personal marketing portfolio that promotes your unique strengths through an authentic, distinctive voice. Your extraordinary qualifications are powerful - allow your true persona to shine through in how they're presented.

Reviewing For Clarity and Simplicity

As you approach the final polish, take a step back and review your entire resume with an eye towards simplicity, clarity and readability. You want your content to be tightly written, direct and free of any confusing jargon or superfluous details.

Some tips for optimizing clarity:
Use Clear, Straightforward Language
Avoid overly complex phrasing, excessive industry jargon or ambiguous language that could confuse readers. Stick to concise, commonly understood terminology as much as possible.

For example, instead of: "Leveraged machine learning techniques to ideate robust algorithmic models for demand forecasting"

Simplify to: "Applied machine learning to build advanced forecasting models increasing demand forecast accuracy by 35%."

Be Judicious With Acronyms

Only use acronyms if they are extremely common/ubiquitous within your industry. Otherwise, spell out the full names/terms to ensure clarity for all readers.

Optimize Content Density and Flow

Break up dense paragraphs or bullets into separate, skimmable sections. Use ample white space to create clear visual separation between distinct details. Adjust ordering to ensure concepts flow logically.

Proofread Meticulously

Thoroughly cross-check for any typos, grammar errors or inconsistent capitalization, abbreviations or numeric formatting. Even minor mistakes can be distracting and erode credibility.

The more you can simplify and streamline your language, the easier it will be for employers to rapidly comprehend your background and qualifications when skimming your resume.

Remember that recruiters frequently have to quickly evaluate hundreds of resumes. You don't want to lose their attention or create any potential confusion with overly complex or wordy content.

Crisp, clear and skimmable writing allows your extraordinary accomplishments to shine in a digestible, hard-hitting way. It promotes your credibility as a candidate and leaves a polished, professional impression.

Seeking Outside Perspective

As you put the final polish on your resume, it can be extremely valuable to get an outside perspective from others. Having a fresh set of eyes review your materials can surface new insights, catch any remaining inconsistencies and validate your messaging resonates as intended.

Some options for soliciting outside feedback:

Leveraging Your Network

Reach out to trusted friends, colleagues, mentors or advisors whose opinion you value. Explain that you're aiming for honest constructive feedback to perfect your resume. Inquire about aspects like:

- Does my personal brand and unique value proposition come through clearly?
- Do any sections need clarification or simplification of language?
- Are there any glaring holes, gaps or inconsistencies I need to address?
- Does the content feel polished, focused and free of errors?
- Does the overall package effectively market me for my target roles?

Just be sure to set expectations that you're looking for candid critiques, not just surface-level praise. Getting thoughtful outside perspectives can be invaluable.

Professional Resume Services

You can also invest in professional resume services or career coaching that includes resume review and optimization. Experienced consultants can provide detailed feedback through the lens of their recruiting expertise.

Many services offer affordable resume critique packages if you just need high-level feedback on your existing materials. Or you can pursue more comprehensive resume rewriting if you need heavier lifting.

Just be cautious of extremely low-cost options that provide only surface-level feedback. And vet any service's credibility by reviewing samples of their prior work.

The key is seeking out experienced, honest third-party perspectives to pressure test your resume and personal brand positioning. An outside expert view can identify potential blindspots and allow you to elevate your materials to the highest level of polish.

With thoughtful external feedback incorporated, you can ensure your extraordinary qualifications and unique differentiators are being marketed with utmost clarity and impact. The final perfected version will put your best professional self forward.

Key Takeaways:
- Thoroughly cross-check every element for consistency in formatting, dates, details and information
- Thoughtfully tailor content to highlight specific qualifications prioritized for roles you're pursuing
- Seamlessly integrate relevant keywords throughout while maintaining natural language

- Address any potential gaps or concerns proactively with honest, empowering context
- Intentionally promote what allows you to stand out through your unique differentiators
- Leverage language and personal anecdotes that capture your authentic brand voice
- Optimize for simplicity, clarity and skimmable readability in your writing
- Solicit outside perspective to pressure test your materials and uncover blindspots

By applying these polishing strategies, you transform your resume from a rough draft into a truly extraordinary, professional masterpiece. Your background and unique value proposition are presented flawlessly.

There are no distracting inconsistencies, vague language or potential gaps left open to interpretation. You've tailored your content to be a precise fit for your current career goals while staying true to your authentic personal brand voice.

Most importantly, you've clearly conveyed what allows you to genuinely differentiate yourself as the ideal candidate for the roles you're targeting. Your extraordinary qualifications shine through compellingly.

With this final polish applied, your resume will make a powerful, cohesive and utterly credible impression on employers from the moment it's opened. You've crafted an intentional, marketing-minded personal portfolio that exudes professionalism.

You can feel confident that your materials will put your best foot forward and represent you with utmost poise throughout the hiring process. You're prepared to speak articulately about your background and handle any follow-up questions that arise.

The journey of resume mastery has involved defining your authentic career narrative, structuring an impactful presentation, showcasing your extraordinary qualifications and now, perfecting every element down to the smallest detail. You've invested the effort to elevate your personal brand and craft truly remarkable career marketing materials.

With this final polish applied, you can move forward sharing your resume and navigating the application process with the self-assurance that you've done everything possible to position yourself for success.

The mastery of perfecting your credentials is the final crucial step that allows you to unlock thrilling new career opportunities aligned with your vision. Your potential is about to be unleashed!

Chapter 6: Complements to Your Written Resume

In today's competitive job market, your written resume is just one piece of the puzzle. To truly stand out and make a lasting impression, you need to complement your resume with additional elements that showcase your unique value proposition. This chapter will explore various strategies and tools that can elevate your job search and help you present a well-rounded, compelling career story.

Personal Branding

Personal branding is the process of creating and managing your unique identity and reputation in the professional world. It involves defining your values, skills, and experiences in a way that sets you apart from others and communicates your value to potential employers.

To define your personal brand, start by reflecting on your strengths, passions, and unique selling points. What makes you stand out from others in your field? What value can you bring to an organization? Once you have a clear understanding of your personal brand, craft a compelling brand statement that succinctly communicates who you are and what you offer.

Ensure that your personal brand aligns with your career goals. If you're seeking a leadership role, for example, your brand should emphasize your management skills and experience. Consistently communicate your brand across all platforms, including your resume, online profiles, and networking interactions.

Social media can be a powerful tool for personal branding. Platforms like LinkedIn, Twitter, and industry-specific forums provide opportunities to showcase your expertise, engage with others in your field, and build your professional reputation. Share relevant content, participate in discussions, and position yourself as a thought leader in your industry.

Online Presence

In addition to social media, your online presence includes your professional website or portfolio, as well as your presence on industry-specific platforms and communities. These digital assets allow you to provide a more comprehensive picture of your skills, experiences, and accomplishments beyond what can be conveyed in a traditional resume.

Optimize your LinkedIn profile by using a professional profile picture, crafting a compelling headline and summary, and highlighting your key skills and experiences. Use the platform to connect with others in your industry, join relevant groups, and engage with content related to your field.

Consider creating a personal website or online portfolio to showcase your work, provide more detail about your experiences, and demonstrate your skills and expertise. This is particularly valuable for professionals in creative fields, such as designers, writers, or developers, but can be beneficial for anyone looking to stand out in their job search.

Engage with industry-specific platforms and communities, such as GitHub for developers or Behance for designers. These platforms provide opportunities to showcase your work, collaborate with others, and build your professional network.

Finally, be mindful of your online reputation. Conduct a Google search of your name to see what information is publicly available, and take steps to manage any negative or unprofessional content. Maintain a consistent, professional presence across all platforms to ensure that your online persona aligns with your personal brand.

Networking

Networking is a critical component of any successful job search. By building relationships with professionals in your industry, you can gain valuable insights, learn about job opportunities, and get your foot in the door with potential employers.

Start by leveraging your existing network, including friends, family, former colleagues, and classmates. Let them know that you're actively seeking new opportunities and ask if they know of any openings or can make introductions to others in your field.

Attend industry events, conferences, and workshops to meet new people and expand your network. Come prepared with business cards and a brief elevator pitch that communicates your personal brand and career goals. Follow up with the contacts you make, expressing your appreciation and reiterating your interest in staying connected.

Effective networking requires a strategic, authentic approach. Focus on building genuine relationships, rather than simply asking for favors or job leads. Offer value to your contacts by sharing relevant articles, making introductions, or providing advice and support when appropriate. Nurture your relationships over time, staying in touch and providing updates on your job search and career progress.

Cover Letters and Application Materials

While your resume provides a snapshot of your qualifications, your cover letter and other application materials offer an opportunity to expand on your experiences, highlight your most relevant skills, and demonstrate your fit for a specific role.

Always tailor your cover letter to the position and company you're applying to. Research the organization and the role, and use your cover letter to communicate how your skills and experiences align with their needs and goals. Use specific examples to illustrate your accomplishments and qualifications, and express your enthusiasm for the opportunity.

In addition to your cover letter, consider including other application materials that can strengthen your candidacy. This might include writing samples, design portfolios, case studies, or project summaries that showcase your skills and achievements. Be selective and strategic in what you choose to include.

Interviewing Skills

Successful interviewing requires preparation, practice, and the ability to articulate your value proposition effectively. Start by researching the company and the specific role you're interviewing for. Understand their mission, values, products or services, and recent news or developments. This knowledge will help you tailor your responses and demonstrate your genuine interest in the opportunity.

Prepare for different types of interviews, such as phone screenings, video interviews, panel interviews, and behavioral or case-based interviews. Each format requires a slightly different approach, so familiarize yourself with the expectations and best practices for each.

Develop a set of compelling stories and examples that highlight your skills, experiences, and accomplishments. Use the STAR method (Situation, Task, Action, Result) to structure your responses, providing concrete examples of how you've demonstrated the qualities and abilities they're seeking.

Practice common interview questions with a friend, family member, or mentor. Ask for feedback on your responses, body language, and overall presentation. The more you practice, the more confident and polished you'll be during the actual interview.

Salary Negotiation

Negotiating salary and benefits can be intimidating, but it's an essential skill for ensuring that you're fairly compensated for your value. Start by researching industry standards and market rates for the role and location. Use resources like Glassdoor, PayScale, and salary surveys to gather data on typical compensation packages.

When discussing salary, focus on your value and the impact you can make in the role, rather than your personal financial needs. Be prepared to justify your desired salary range with specific examples of your skills, experience, and past successes.

Consider non-monetary benefits as well, such as flexible work arrangements, professional development opportunities, or additional vacation time. These factors can significantly impact your overall job satisfaction and work-life balance.

Approach salary negotiations with confidence and a collaborative mindset. Be willing to listen to the employer's perspective and find mutually beneficial solutions. If an offer doesn't meet your expectations, propose alternative compensation packages or ask about the potential for future performance-based bonuses or raises.

Post-Interview Follow-Up

After an interview, it's crucial to follow up with a thank-you note expressing your gratitude for the opportunity and reiterating your interest in the position. Use this message to highlight key points from your conversation, address any outstanding questions or concerns, and reinforce your relevant skills and experiences.

If you don't hear back within the expected timeframe, follow up politely to inquire about the status of your application. Maintain a positive, professional tone, and avoid appearing impatient or aggressive.

Even if you don't receive a job offer, maintain a gracious and professional demeanor. Thank the employer for their time and consideration, and express your continued interest in future opportunities with the company. A positive attitude can leave a lasting impression and may lead to other opportunities down the line.

Continuous Professional Development

To remain competitive in your field and advance your career, it's essential to continuously invest in your professional development. Identify areas where you can improve your skills or knowledge, and seek out opportunities to learn and grow.

Attend industry conferences, workshops, and seminars to stay up-to-date on the latest trends and best practices. Pursue relevant certifications or training programs to expand your skill set and demonstrate your commitment to your profession.

Seek feedback and mentorship from colleagues, supervisors, or industry experts. Ask for constructive criticism on your work, and be open to suggestions for improvement. Building relationships with mentors can provide valuable guidance, support, and opportunities for growth.

Stay engaged with your professional community by participating in online forums, contributing to industry publications, or volunteering for leadership roles in relevant organizations. These activities can help you build your reputation, expand your network, and gain valuable experience.

By consistently focusing on your professional development, you'll be better equipped to adapt to changing industry demands, take on new challenges, and advance your career over the long term.

Conclusion

Complementing your written resume with a strong personal brand, online presence, networking skills, and tailored application materials can significantly enhance your job search success. By developing your interviewing skills, negotiating effectively, and maintaining professional relationships, you'll be well-positioned to navigate the hiring process and secure the opportunities you desire.

Remember that your career development is an ongoing journey. By continuously investing in your skills, knowledge, and professional network, you'll be able to adapt to new challenges, seize exciting opportunities, and achieve your long-term career goals.
As you implement the strategies and techniques covered in this chapter, keep in mind that authenticity and consistency are key. Ensure that your personal brand, online presence, and application materials accurately reflect your unique strengths,

experiences, and career goals. Consistency across all platforms and interactions reinforces your credibility and professionalism.

As you implement the strategies and techniques covered in this chapter, keep in mind that authenticity and consistency are key. Ensure that your personal brand, online presence, and application materials accurately reflect your unique strengths, experiences, and career goals. Consistency across all platforms and interactions reinforces your credibility and professionalism.

Building a strong professional network takes time and effort, but the benefits are invaluable. Nurture your relationships by providing value, expressing gratitude, and maintaining regular contact. A robust network can open doors to new opportunities, provide valuable advice and support, and help you navigate challenges throughout your career.

When applying and interviewing for positions, tailor your approach to each specific opportunity. Demonstrate your genuine interest and enthusiasm by researching the company and role, asking thoughtful questions, and highlighting how your skills and experiences align with their needs.

Negotiating salary and benefits can be challenging, but it's an essential part of advocating for your worth and ensuring fair compensation. Approach these conversations with confidence, preparation, and a collaborative mindset. Remember that negotiation is a two-way process, and be open to finding mutually beneficial solutions.

Finally, embrace a mindset of continuous learning and growth. The professional landscape is constantly evolving, and staying adaptable and proactive in your development is crucial for long-term success. Seek out new challenges, take on stretch assignments, and invest in your skills and knowledge. By consistently pushing yourself outside of your comfort zone, you'll be better equipped to seize new opportunities and advance your career.

In summary, leveraging the power of personal branding, networking, and strategic job search techniques can help you stand out in a competitive market and achieve your professional goals. By presenting a cohesive, compelling career narrative across all touchpoints, you'll be able to effectively showcase your unique value proposition and land the opportunities you desire.

Remember, your career journey is a marathon, not a sprint. Stay focused on your long-term objectives, while remaining adaptable and open to new possibilities. By consistently investing in your professional development, building strong relationships, and showcasing your skills and experiences, you'll be well-positioned for ongoing growth and success.

As you embark on this next chapter of your career, approach each opportunity with enthusiasm, authenticity, and a commitment to excellence. Your unique talents, experiences, and perspective have the power to make a significant impact in your chosen field. Embrace your strengths, learn from your challenges, and never stop striving for your goals.

With the strategies and insights provided in this guide, you have the tools and knowledge needed to take your career to new heights. Trust in your abilities, stay true to your values, and approach your professional journey with confidence and purpose. Your future is bright, and your potential is limitless. Go forth and create the career of your dreams!

Key Takeaways:
1. Personal branding: Define your unique identity and reputation by reflecting on your strengths, passions, and value proposition. Craft a compelling brand statement and communicate it consistently across all platforms.

2. Online presence: Optimize your LinkedIn profile, create a personal website or portfolio, engage with industry-specific platforms, and manage your online reputation to provide a comprehensive picture of your skills and experiences.
3. Networking: Build relationships with professionals in your industry by leveraging your existing network, attending events, and offering value to your contacts. Focus on building genuine relationships and nurturing them over time.
4. Cover letters and application materials: Tailor your cover letter to the position and company, using specific examples to illustrate your qualifications. Include additional materials like writing samples or portfolios to strengthen your candidacy.
5. Interviewing skills: Research the company and role, prepare compelling stories using the STAR method, practice common questions, and be confident in articulating your value proposition.
6. Salary negotiation: Research industry standards, focus on your value and impact, consider non-monetary benefits, and approach negotiations with a collaborative mindset.
7. Post-interview follow-up: Send a thank-you note, reiterate your interest, and maintain a positive, professional demeanor even if you don't receive an offer.
8. Continuous professional development: Invest in your skills and knowledge through conferences, workshops, certifications, seeking feedback, and engaging with your professional community.
9. Authenticity and consistency: Ensure your personal brand, online presence, and application materials accurately reflect your unique strengths and career goals.
10. Building relationships: Nurture your professional network by providing value, expressing gratitude, and maintaining regular contact to open doors to new opportunities and support throughout your career.

Chapter 7: Navigating the Job Application Process

You've invested significant effort into defining your authentic career narrative, crafting an extraordinary resume that markets your unique value proposition, and developing a rich portfolio of complementary personal branding materials.

Now that you've mastered the art of positioning your extraordinary credentials, it's time to leverage those assets strategically to navigate the entire job application and hiring process with poise and confidence.

In this final chapter, you'll gain proven strategies for customizing your materials for each specific opportunity you pursue. You'll learn best practices for submitting applications, conducting proactive outreach, and following up effectively to increase your chances of moving forward.

From there, you'll explore advanced techniques for interviewing with intention - how to reinforce your personal brand, articulate key accomplishments with impact, and navigate the negotiation process to land offers aligned with your goals.

By applying a comprehensive, end-to-end approach that extends beyond just your initial resume, you'll be able to propel your extraordinary qualifications throughout every stage of your professional journey. You'll be equipped to unlock exciting new roles and continue advancing your career with confidence and momentum.

Customizing Application Materials Purposefully

While your core resume provides an overview of your credentials, it's important to customize components like your cover letter and any other application materials to speak directly to the unique requirements of each specific role you're pursuing.

As you prepare to apply for an open position, take time to thoroughly review and deconstruct the job description to understand the key qualifications, skills and responsibilities they're seeking. Research the company's culture, values, products/services and any other relevant context.

Then, thoughtfully tailor the following elements:

Cover Letter
- Opening line that conveys your distinct value prop for this role
- Specific accomplishments and skills that align to their requirements
- Knowledge of the company/role that demonstrates intentionality
- Personal motivations or mission alignment that reinforces fit

Resume
- Update your summary/objective to integrate relevant keywords
- Reorder and tweak experience bullets to elevate most applicable accomplishments
- Adjust skills lists and other sections to mirror the job description's language
- Incorporate any accomplishments that exemplify required skills

Portfolio Samples
- Curate any work samples, reports or multimedia examples that prove mastery of the core competencies required - customize as a focused "highlights reel" for this role.

The key is ensuring your application goes beyond generic, one-size-fits-all documents. You'll want every component to speak precisely to how your extraordinary qualifications can fulfill this role's needs and drive impact for this specific company's priorities.

Avoid reusing stale materials or taking a scattershot approach of blasting generic resumes. Thoughtful customization conveys your intentionality as a candidate and allows you to control the narrative around your fit.

Conducting Strategic Outreach and Follow-Up

Beyond simply applying to open job postings, you can increase your odds of getting noticed by conducting strategic outreach to individuals and companies you're interested in. This proactive approach allows you to get ahead of the competition and make lasting connections.

When reaching out about potential opportunities, customize your message for each specific person/company you're targeting. Reference any mutual connections or explain why you're interested in their organization. And be sure to include your tailored resume as well as links to your online portfolio/credentials.

Some best practices for effective outreach:
- Focus on quality over quantity - identify 5-10 companies per week to reach out to directly
- Leverage LinkedIn's alumni tools to connect with employees who went to your university
- Ask for brief informational interviews to learn more about their roles/culture
- Follow up politely 1-2 times if you don't receive an initial response
- Track your outreach efforts so you can follow up on any leads that emerge over time

Even if companies don't have any open roles currently, getting your extraordinary credentials on their radar can pay off down the line. You'll be top-of-mind when new positions do open up.

It's also valuable to set Google Alerts or enable LinkedIn job notification preferences to be automatically informed of relevant new openings that you can then apply to rapidly.

The key is maintaining a consistent cadence of strategic outreach and follow-up as you navigate your job search. This proactive approach allows you to expand your opportunities while reinforcing your personal brand as a motivated, driven candidate.

Mastering the Interview Process

Once your strategic outreach generates interviews, it's crucial to approach each one as an opportunity to bring your compelling career narrative to life. Proper preparation and an intentional mindset are key.

Prior to each interview, thoroughly research the company, role responsibilities, and backgrounds of the people interviewing you. Identify specific examples from your experience that you can articulate to showcase your qualifications. Have thoughtful questions prepared to demonstrate your enthusiasm and intentionality about this particular opportunity.

During the interview itself, start by reiterating your personal value proposition and motivations for the role. This anchors the narrative you want to convey. Then, tell engaging stories around your key accomplishments that illustrate how you've applied the specific skills they are seeking. Emphasize how your experience aligns with their priorities.

Don't just respond to questions - intentionally guide the conversation to reinforce your distinct qualifications. The interview is your chance to control the narrative and substantiate why you are an ideal fit.

Insightful questions you ask the interviewers also allow you to evaluate if the role and company align with your goals while conveying your proactivity. Gather insights to inform your own decision process.

After the interview, promptly follow up with personal thank you notes reiterating your interest and recapping how your strengths can contribute. This reinforces your memorable personal brand one last time.

By approaching interviews with poise, intentionality and an emphasis on your authentic career narrative, you increase your chances of advancing and receiving offers aligned with your aspirations.

Evaluating Offers & Negotiating Effectively

As you progress through the hiring process, you may receive job offers requiring careful evaluation and negotiation. Approach this phase with the same brand-driven mindset and professionalism.

If you receive an offer, thank the employer and request a reasonable timeframe to thoroughly consider it, unless you are completely certain you want to accept. This allows you to carefully review all components like compensation, benefits, responsibilities, company culture and growth potential. Identify any areas that may need clarification or negotiation.

When negotiating, do so respectfully while advocating for an equitable deal. Explain your rationale for any adjustments calmly, using data-driven benchmarks if appropriate. You can reinforce your interest and fit while still ensuring the opportunity aligns fully with your goals.

If you opt to decline an offer, handle it graciously. Reiterate your gratitude for the opportunity while explaining your reasoned decision with professionalism and transparency.

No matter the outcome, approach each step with intentionality and poise. Continually reinforce the compelling narrative around your extraordinary value through every interaction. By staying true to your personal brand, you optimize your ability to secure opportunities aligned with your priorities.

The job search process is a multi-stage journey. But by applying a comprehensive, brand-driven strategy at each phase - from customized application materials to strategic networking, memorable interviews and principled negotiations - you maximize your chances of achieving your desired outcome. Your authentic career narrative remains the guiding force for your professional trajectory.

Sustaining Professional Momentum

Securing an exciting new role aligned with your goals is a significant accomplishment. However, it's important to sustain your professional growth momentum even after starting your next position. Continually nurturing your personal brand narrative and portfolio of accomplishments will position you for future career advancement.

Once you've begun a new job, identify high-visibility projects and stretch opportunities that allow you to make an impact quickly. Pursue initiatives that expand your skills and experiences so you can accumulate new success stories to add to your portfolio. Document your contributions meticulously.

Stay attuned to your company's priorities, challenges and broader industry trends. Look for ways to innovate and drive valuable initiatives forward as a thought leader. Write, speak or develop intellectual property related to your expertise.

Cultivate strong collaborative relationships by taking a genuine interest in your colleagues' roles and responsibilities. An inclusive leadership style will make you a respected team player.

Proactively seek feedback from managers and mentors on areas for improvement. Use that input to continually refine your skills and identify professional development areas to focus on next. Maintain a growth mindset.

As you achieve new accomplishments, update your resume, LinkedIn profile and other career marketing materials regularly. Don't let your portfolio become stale - evolve your personal brand narrative to reflect your latest extraordinary achievements.

This consistent professional growth mindset enhances your visibility while keeping you marketable for future opportunities that may arise, even if you don't have imminent plans to pursue them.

Maintaining momentum safeguards your long-term career prospects and positions you for future transitions from a position of strength and differentiation. Your personal brand remains your prime professional asset and competitive edge.

By nurturing it intentionally at every stage - from landing a new role, to driving impact, to continually showcasing your evolving qualifications - you can maximize your ability to keep unlocking fulfilling experiences and impact over your entire career trajectory.

Advancing Your Career With Intention

As you progress through various roles and career experiences, it's important to periodically reassess your professional goals and aspirations. Your personal brand narrative should evolve alongside your ambitions to ensure you remain intentionally aligned.

Take time every few years to reflect on your motivations, values, and desired legacy. How have your interests or priorities shifted? What new experiences or credentials are you seeking to develop? Revisit and refine your overarching career narrative to capture this evolution.

Identify any skills gaps you need to fill or certifications to obtain to qualify for more advanced roles. Pursue educational opportunities, training programs or specializations that allow you to upskill proactively. Staying ahead of emerging trends enhances your marketability.

If you're feeling stagnant in your current role, have honest conversations with your manager about taking on new responsibilities or lateraling into different positions that reignite your growth. Complacency can stall your momentum.

You may also decide that your long-term goals require making an external career transition to a different company, industry or entrepreneurial path. In these cases, reactivate your job search strategies - networking strategically, updating application materials, interviewing intentionally.

No matter which direction you pursue, approach it with the same focused personal branding mindset you originally cultivated. Craft an updated career narrative that conveys your evolving value proposition and unique qualifications for these new opportunities.

Maintain a portfolio that markets your latest accomplishments, thought leadership, skills and credentials. Update your resume, online profiles and materials so you're continually promoting your extraordinary professional progression.

At every new phase, be prepared to articulate how your motivations, experiences and vision align with these elevated roles. Guide each conversation and interaction to reinforce your aspirational personal brand narrative.

The journey of fulfilling your ambitions doesn't have a final destination - it's a continuous cycle of intentional growth and evolution. By persistently nurturing your authentic career narrative, you equip yourself to keep navigating upward and achieving greater impact with clarity and confidence.

Maximizing Your Interview Performance
Once you've successfully captured the attention of potential employers through your well-crafted application materials, the next crucial step is to excel during the interview process. Interviews provide an invaluable opportunity to showcase your unique qualifications, personality, and fit for the role. By approaching interviews with the same level of intention and preparation as your written materials, you can differentiate yourself as an extraordinary candidate.

Research and Preparation

Before each interview, conduct thorough research on the company, its mission, values, and recent developments. Familiarize yourself with the specific role requirements and how your skills align. This knowledge will allow you to tailor your responses and demonstrate genuine interest in the opportunity.

Anticipate common interview questions and practice articulating your answers out loud. Prepare specific examples and anecdotes that illustrate your relevant experiences, achievements, and lessons learned. Rehearsing your responses builds confidence and helps you communicate your value proposition concisely and compellingly.

Conveying Your Personal Brand

During the interview, seize every opportunity to reinforce your personal brand narrative. Weave your unique story, motivations, and vision into your responses. Share examples that highlight your defining strengths, transferable skills, and capacity for impact.

Be prepared to discuss how your values and aspirations align with the company's mission and culture. Express your enthusiasm for contributing to their goals and making a meaningful difference. Demonstrating a strong connection between your personal brand and the organization's priorities sets you apart as an ideal fit.

Engaging in Authentic Dialogue

While interviews are an opportunity to sell yourself, approach them as a two-way conversation. Ask thoughtful questions that demonstrate your genuine curiosity and desire to understand the role, team dynamics, and growth opportunities. Engage the interviewer in authentic dialogue to build rapport and gain deeper insights.

Listen attentively to the information shared and adapt your responses accordingly. Show flexibility in your thinking and a willingness to learn and collaborate. By creating a dynamic, reciprocal exchange, you leave a memorable impression of your unique personality and potential.

Following Up with Impact

After each interview, send a timely and personalized thank-you note to express your appreciation for the opportunity. Reiterate your enthusiasm for the role and highlight any key points from the conversation that reinforced your fit. This gesture shows professionalism and keeps you top of mind as a standout candidate.

If you don't receive a response within the expected timeframe, follow up politely to inquire about the status of your application. Persistence demonstrates your continued interest and commitment to the opportunity.

By approaching interviews with the same level of intentionality as your written materials, you can consistently communicate your extraordinary value proposition. Thorough preparation, authentic engagement, and timely follow-up will differentiate you as a candidate who not only possesses the required qualifications but also aligns seamlessly with the company's mission and culture. Excel in your interviews to propel your career journey forward with confidence and impact.

Negotiating Offers and Making Strategic Decisions

Receiving a job offer is an exciting milestone in your career journey. It validates the strength of your qualifications and the impact of your personal branding efforts. However, before accepting an offer, it's essential to approach the negotiation process with the same level of intention and strategic thinking you've applied throughout your job search.

Evaluating Compensation and Benefits

Carefully review the compensation package, including base salary, bonuses, stock options, and benefits. Research industry benchmarks and market rates for similar roles to ensure the offer aligns with your expectations and value. Consider your personal financial goals and lifestyle requirements when assessing the adequacy of the package.

If the initial offer falls short of your expectations, prepare to negotiate respectfully. Gather data points and specific examples that justify your request for higher compensation or additional benefits. Approach the conversation with professionalism and a collaborative mindset, focusing on finding a mutually beneficial agreement.

Assessing Career Growth and Development

Beyond financial considerations, evaluate the potential for long-term career growth and development within the organization. Inquire about opportunities for advancement, skill acquisition, and leadership roles. Assess whether the company's trajectory aligns with your aspirations and if there is a clear path for your continued professional evolution.

Consider the mentorship, training, and development programs available to support your growth. Evaluate the company's commitment to employee development and whether it provides the resources and support necessary for you to thrive and make a lasting impact.

Aligning with Company Culture and Values

Before accepting an offer, reflect on the company's culture, values, and mission. Assess whether they align with your own beliefs, work style, and long-term goals. A strong cultural fit is crucial for your overall job satisfaction, productivity, and ability to make meaningful contributions.

Consider the team dynamics, communication style, and leadership philosophy of your potential manager and colleagues. Evaluate whether the work environment fosters collaboration, innovation, and inclusivity. A company that aligns with your values and supports your authentic self will enable you to perform at your best and find fulfillment in your work.

Making a Strategic Decision

Once you've thoroughly evaluated the offer and conducted necessary negotiations, it's time to make a strategic decision. Reflect on how accepting the role aligns with your overarching career narrative and long-term objectives. Consider whether it represents a logical next step in your professional journey and if it positions you for the impact and growth you seek.

Trust your instincts and weigh the potential risks and rewards. If the opportunity aligns with your goals, values, and aspirations, confidently accept the offer and prepare to embark on an exciting new chapter in your career.

Navigating the job application process with intention requires a comprehensive approach that extends beyond crafting compelling materials. By excelling in interviews, negotiating offers strategically, and making decisions that align with your long-term vision, you position yourself for success and fulfillment in your chosen career path. Embrace each stage of the process as an opportunity to showcase your unique value proposition and take purposeful steps towards realizing your professional aspirations.

Maintaining Momentum and Adapting to Change

As you successfully navigate the job application process and embark on new career opportunities, it's crucial to maintain the momentum you've built and adapt to the inevitable changes that come with professional growth. Your personal brand is not a static entity but rather an evolving representation of your skills, experiences, and aspirations. By consistently nurturing your brand and embracing a mindset of continuous learning and adaptation, you position yourself for long-term success and resilience.

Staying Current and Relevant

In today's rapidly evolving business landscape, staying current and relevant is essential to maintaining your competitive edge. Regularly update your skills and knowledge through ongoing learning and professional development. Attend industry conferences, workshops, and webinars to stay informed about emerging trends, technologies, and best practices in your field.

Engage in continuous self-reflection and assess how your experiences and accomplishments shape your evolving personal brand narrative. Regularly update your resume, online profiles, and portfolio to showcase your latest achievements, skills, and thought leadership. By consistently demonstrating your commitment to growth and relevance, you reinforce your value proposition and attract new opportunities aligned with your goals.

Building and Nurturing Your Network

Your professional network is a valuable asset in navigating career transitions and uncovering new opportunities. Continuously expand and nurture your network by actively engaging with colleagues, mentors, and industry peers. Attend networking events, join professional associations, and participate in online forums and discussions relevant to your field.

Cultivate meaningful relationships by offering value, sharing insights, and supporting others in their professional journeys. Maintain regular contact with your network, even when you're not actively seeking new opportunities. By establishing yourself as a trusted and supportive member of your professional community, you create a strong foundation for future collaborations and career advancement.

Embracing Change and Adaptability

Change is an inevitable part of any career journey, and embracing adaptability is key to thriving in the face of uncertainty. Be open to new opportunities, even if they deviate from your original plan. Embrace challenges as chances to learn, grow, and demonstrate your resilience.

When faced with unexpected setbacks or transitions, reframe them as opportunities to reassess your goals and chart a new course. Adapt your personal brand narrative to highlight how your experiences and lessons learned have shaped your unique perspective and strengthened your ability to navigate change.

Cultivate a growth mindset, viewing obstacles as opportunities for learning and development. Seek out mentors and advisors who can provide guidance and support during times of transition. By approaching change with a positive and proactive attitude, you demonstrate your adaptability and position yourself for continued success.

Conclusion

Navigating the job application process with intention is a transformative journey that extends beyond landing your next role. By crafting a compelling personal brand, excelling in interviews, negotiating strategically, and making decisions aligned with your long-term vision, you lay the foundation for a fulfilling and impactful career.

Maintain the momentum you've built by staying current, nurturing your network, and embracing adaptability in the face of change. Your personal brand is a powerful tool for communicating your unique value proposition and attracting opportunities that align with your evolving goals and aspirations.

Remember, your career journey is an ongoing process of self-discovery, growth, and impact. By approaching each stage with intention, authenticity, and a commitment to continuous learning, you position yourself for long-term success and fulfillment. Embrace the challenges and opportunities that lie ahead, and trust in your ability to navigate the path towards your envisioned future.

Key Takeaways:
1. Maximizing Your Interview Performance
    - Conduct thorough research on the company and role before each interview
    - Prepare specific examples and anecdotes that highlight your relevant experiences and achievements
    - Reinforce your personal brand narrative throughout the interview
    - Engage in authentic dialogue and ask thoughtful questions
    - Follow up with a timely and personalized thank-you note

2. Negotiating Offers and Making Strategic Decisions
    - Evaluate compensation packages against industry benchmarks and personal financial goals
    - Negotiate respectfully, using data points and examples to justify requests
    - Assess potential for long-term career growth and development within the organization
    - Consider alignment with company culture, values, and mission
    - Make strategic decisions based on alignment with overarching career narrative and long-term objectives
3. Maintaining Momentum and Adapting to Change
    - Stay current and relevant through ongoing learning and professional development
    - Regularly update resume, online profiles, and portfolio to showcase latest achievements and skills
    - Build and nurture professional network through active engagement and offering value
    - Embrace change and adaptability, viewing challenges as opportunities for growth
    - Cultivate a growth mindset and seek guidance from mentors during times of transition
4. Approaching the Job Application Process with Intention
    - Craft a compelling personal brand that communicates unique value proposition
    - Excel in interviews by preparing thoroughly and engaging authentically
    - Negotiate offers strategically, considering both financial and career growth aspects
    - Make decisions aligned with long-term vision and aspirations
    - Maintain momentum by staying current, nurturing network, and embracing adaptability
5. Embracing the Career Journey

- View career journey as an ongoing process of self-discovery, growth, and impact
- Approach each stage with intention, authenticity, and commitment to continuous learning
- Trust in ability to navigate challenges and opportunities towards envisioned future
- Continuously refine and adapt personal brand narrative to reflect evolving goals and experiences

By keeping these key takeaways in mind, professionals can navigate the job application process with intention, maximize their impact, and achieve long-term career success and fulfillment. Embracing the journey with a growth mindset and adaptability positions individuals to thrive in an ever-evolving professional landscape.

Conclusion

Throughout this book, we've explored the art and science of crafting an extraordinary resume that authentically markets your unique skills, experiences, and potential. By mastering the strategies and mindset shifts outlined in these chapters, you're now equipped with a powerful toolkit to create a compelling career narrative that opens doors to exciting opportunities.

We began by laying the foundation of defining your distinctive career story through self-assessment and personal branding. You learned to identify your core strengths, accomplishments, and value proposition, which serve as the bedrock for all your professional marketing materials.

Next, we dove into the structural and formatting elements that make your resume visually impactful and reader-friendly. By optimizing each section for clarity and relevance, you can ensure that your qualifications shine through and capture the attention of both human readers and applicant tracking systems.

The heart of resume mastery lies in transforming your work experiences into compelling evidence of your abilities. By crafting high-impact achievement statements that quantify and qualify your contributions, you can paint a vivid picture of the value you bring to any organization. We explored techniques for highlighting transferable skills, tailoring your content to specific roles, and creating a cohesive narrative that positions you as an ideal candidate.

Beyond the core resume, we examined complementary tools like cover letters, LinkedIn profiles, and personal websites that allow you to reinforce your professional brand across multiple touchpoints. By leveraging these resources strategically, you can create a powerful ecosystem of self-marketing materials that amplify your strengths and set you apart from the competition.

Finally, we provided a roadmap for navigating the entire job application process with intention and confidence. From customizing your materials for each opportunity to acing interviews and negotiating offers, you now have a comprehensive approach to position yourself optimally at every stage of your career journey.

Remember, resume mastery is not a one-time event but an ongoing process of self-discovery, adaptation, and growth. As you continue to evolve professionally, so too should your resume and personal branding. By regularly updating your materials to reflect your latest achievements, skills, and aspirations, you can ensure that your career story remains dynamic and relevant in an ever-changing landscape.

The journey to resume excellence is ultimately one of empowerment – over how you're perceived, the opportunities you attract, and your ability to achieve the career you envision. By taking ownership of your professional narrative and marketing yourself with authenticity and impact, you become the architect of your own success.

As you embark on the next chapter of your career armed with the tools and mindset of resume mastery, remember to approach the process with courage, resilience, and a commitment to continuous learning. Embrace the power of your unique story, and trust in your ability to navigate the path towards a fulfilling and rewarding professional future.

Your extraordinary resume is more than just a document – it's a catalyst for unlocking your true potential and achieving the career of your dreams. So go forth with confidence, knowing that you have the skills and strategies to captivate employers and propel your career to new heights. The world is waiting for the distinctive value that only you can offer. Let your resume be the key that opens the door to a lifetime of professional success and satisfaction.

Epilogue: Your Career Journey Continues

Congratulations on completing this comprehensive guide to crafting an extraordinary resume and navigating the job application process with intention. By absorbing the strategies, techniques, and mindset shifts outlined in these chapters, you've taken a significant step towards unlocking your full potential and achieving the career of your dreams.

However, your journey doesn't end here. In fact, it's just the beginning. As you move forward with your newly minted resume and a arsenal of self-marketing tools, remember that your career is an ongoing story that continues to unfold with each new experience, skill, and accomplishment.

The key to long-term success lies in embracing a mindset of continuous growth and adaptation. Just as the job market evolves, so too must your approach to presenting yourself as a candidate. By regularly reassessing your goals, updating your materials, and seeking out new opportunities to learn and develop, you can ensure that your career narrative remains fresh, relevant, and compelling.

Remember, your resume is a living document that should grow and change alongside you. Don't be afraid to revisit and refine your content as you gain new insights, experiences, and achievements. Each iteration of your resume is an opportunity to showcase your progress and reaffirm your unique value proposition.

As you embark on future job searches, interviews, and career transitions, carry with you the confidence and self-awareness that comes from having a deep understanding of your own story. Trust in the power of your authentic voice and the impact of your contributions. Your resume is a testament to the skills, talents, and passion that you bring to every professional endeavor.

Beyond the tactical aspects of resume writing and job applications, never lose sight of the bigger picture – your career journey is ultimately a reflection of your personal growth and evolution. Embrace the challenges and opportunities that come your way as chances to learn, adapt, and thrive. Surround yourself with mentors, colleagues, and resources that support your development and inspire you to reach for new heights.

Remember, your career is not a destination but a journey of continuous self-discovery and impact. By approaching each stage with intention, resilience, and a commitment to your own growth, you'll be well-equipped to navigate the twists and turns of your professional path with grace and purpose.

So as you close this book and step forward into the next chapter of your career, do so with the knowledge that you have the tools, mindset, and capacity to craft an extraordinary story – one resume, one opportunity, one achievement at a time. The world is waiting for the unique talents and contributions that only you can offer. Go forth and make your mark, knowing that your journey to professional fulfillment is always just beginning.

Your resume mastery is a launching pad for a lifetime of success, growth, and impact. Embrace the adventure ahead, and trust in your ability to create a career story that inspires, empowers, and opens doors to a future beyond your wildest dreams. The blank page awaits – it's time to write your next chapter.

www.ingramcontent.com/pod-product-compliance
Lightning Source LLC
Chambersburg PA
CBHW062108220526
45471CB00010B/3651